Praise f
Hollyhocks and G

"*Donnerwetter noch einmal!* That's what my mother's mother used to say to my sister and me when we pushed too close to the edge of her patience. Lucy Bertha Ida Christoph, who married a Norwegian American, was a daughter of German immigrants, but not Germans from Russia. Still, the phrase connects us. The *Schwäbisch* or Low German words and phrases sprinkled throughout this book flavor it with sounds and meanings of the Old Country, the one people had left to move to various parts of the Russian Empire around the beginning of the nineteenth century. Pulling up stakes again they moved to America, to the Upper Midwest, and continued to farm and to lead church-centered lives, raising large families and cooking distinctive foods.

Language, food, family, chores, weather, school, holidays, church – nostalgic elements of childhood in Germans from Russia communities in North Dakota, South Dakota, Kansas, Canada, and Minnesota. All are reflected in this volume of prose and verse memories. This isn't the place for sad or scary stories, although having to climb back on the corn planter after the horses ran away can't have been much fun. One author got it right: homesteaders are more important than grasshoppers. These homesteaders didn't let grasshoppers drive them away!"

Deborah L. Miller, Reference Specialist,
Minnesota Historical Society

"This impressive collection provides a kaleidoscope of childhood memories and poems in the voice of German from Russia descendants whose ancestors left their German villages in South Russia and settled the Northern Plains in the last quarter of the nineteenth century and first decades of the twentieth century. Kudos to Minnesota's North Star Chapter, Germans from Russia, for inspiring their members to share their memories with the rest of us."

Michael M. Miller, Director & Bibliographer,
Germans from Russia Heritage Collection, NDSU Libraries, Fargo, ND

"All things German Russian are contained here—rock-picking and kuchen-making and root cellars and country school and fleischküchle and brauche and back-breaking work in the fields and meadowlarks and butchering and church-going and hochzeits and wedding schnapps. These things were so ubiquitous to many German Russian childhoods that it would have been impossible to imagine life being any different. And now it is, so different.

To grow up German Russian was to be taught by one's elders to aim yourself forward, into the future, into hard work, America, and assimilation. The authors whose work is contained in *Hollyhocks and Grasshoppers* have willfully disobeyed that forward command for this short time. They have looked back with intensity and real mastery to conjure up that lost world that lives quietly within those of us who grew up German Russian. Their backward gaze is joyful and full of longing. Each sentence, each line here rings with honesty and empathy, understanding and, most of all, love."

Debra Marquart, author of
The Horizontal World: Growing up Wild in the Middle of Nowhere

"What a wonderful conversation! The authors are a congregation of individuals discovering that they are part of something big, a shared remembrance that makes them Germans from Russia. Their conversation is full of things of the senses, sweet and sweaty, and it is utterly authentic."

Dr. Tom Isern, Professor of History,
North Dakota State University

Best wishes
from Jim Gessele
10/25/14

HOLLYHOCKS *and* GRASSHOPPERS

BEST WISHES

John K. Holzer
SEE PAGE 85

Hertha Bieber Lutz
see pg 47 50

Milt -
Thanks for visiting!
Thanks for
sharing your story!
Cynthia Miller
10/25/14

Nancy Gutner

HOLLYHOCKS *and*
GRASSHOPPERS

Growing Up German *from*
Russia *in* America

 NORTH STAR CHAPTER
OF MINNESOTA
Germans from Russia

To the members of the
North Star Chapter of Minnesota
(Germans from Russia)

Mill City Press, Inc.
322 First Avenue N, 5th floor
Minneapolis, MN 55401
612.455.2293
www.millcitypublishing.com

Cover Art by Virginia Weispfenning Peterson, Used with permission

ISBN-13: 978-1-62652-549-8
LCCN: 013920766

Cover Design by James Arneson
Typeset by Kristeen Ott

Printed in the United States of America

ACKNOWLEDGMENTS

Many thanks:

- to the members of the North Star Chapter of Minnesota (Germans from Russia) who shared their poems, essays, photographs and publishing funds
- to Virginia Weispfenning Peterson for providing cover art entitled "Golden Suncured Grasses"
- to Jim Gessele for assistance with dialect phrases
- to Paul Maggitti for technical support

Table of Contents:

FOREWORD

Book Committee at work. From left: Cindy Miller, Bernie Becker, Carol Just, Nancy Gertner, Sharon Chmielarz. (Photo courtesy of Paul Maggitti)

Making this book has been like putting together a quilt. The theme – what it was like growing up German from Russia – required the stories from many voices. We laid the stories on the table like quilt pieces. We needed to shape them as shared experience, to see where and how the stories' pieces would match to make their own pattern on the given theme. We read and edited, stitched and re-stitched, until the pattern was as complete as we could make it.

And speaking of work, a four-letter word that Germans from Russia easily relate to, this book praises our ancestors for living with unrelenting daily labor. Today we may struggle with computer crashes and an e-machine life, but in the past old and young wrestled with teams of horses, plagues, hunger, monster weather, and surviving voyages across great expanses to gamble hopefully on the unknown.

From that comes this book's title: *Hollyhocks and Grasshoppers: Growing up German from Russia in America*. The hollyhocks represent the hopes and desire for simple beauty which we bring with us, seeds for the future. The grasshoppers represent the new challenges and hardships our ancestors overcame in this new country.

We hope you'll enjoy reading this book, that your day will be enriched by it. You'll find stories here that introduce you to *how it was* or recall for you *how it was* in a past that we want to pass on to you before it's forgotten.

The Editors:
Bernelda Kallenberger Becker
Sharon Grenz Chmielarz
Nancy Gertner
Carol Just
Cynthia Miller

Note to Readers

What does it mean to be a German from Russia in America?

Basically it means that we descend from migrating ancestors who were German-dialect speakers. Many were farmers who risked change and were willing to set down roots where they could practice their religion, keep their language, and live a peaceful, agrarian life.

When the former German Princess, Czarina Catherine the Great, and later her grandson, Czar Alexander I, wanted to settle lands along the Volga River region (1763) and the region of the Black Sea (1802), they offered an enticing deal to our German ancestors who were looking for more land and peace, wanting to avoid wars that claimed taxes, crops, livestock, and worst of all, conscripted their sons to military service.

To migrate to Russia, our ancestors were expected to have skills in viniculture, livestock breeding, and have good farm and trade management skills. In addition to free land, they were allowed to keep their language, be self-governing, exercise religious freedom, and were exempt from military service. German colonists established hundreds of villages along the Volga River region and in the Black Sea area of South Russia. The first years were filled with hardship and mortality rates were high, but with hard work and perseverance, agriculture as well as business and viniculture thrived.

Once established, life was good for Germans in Russia until June 1871, when Czar Alexander II cancelled all rights and privileges granted to the German colonists. Schools were to be "Russified," German colonies were given Russian names and were no longer self governed. Perhaps worst of all, the sons of the colonists were required to serve in the Czar's army.

Meanwhile in America, President Abraham Lincoln signed the Homestead Act of 1862, opening vast spaces of virgin soil to homesteaders. Many of our ancestors migrated once again in search of a life with the freedoms they valued.

German colonists in Russia began leaving in significant numbers in the 1870s and migrated to North and South America, settling in Canada, the United States, Mexico, Argentina, and Brazil. Some chose to homestead in Dakota Territory, Iowa, Minnesota, Kansas, Oklahoma, and Nebraska. Others worked on the railroads in Nebraska and the sugar beet fields in Colorado and western Nebraska. Factory jobs lured them to Sheboygan or Racine, Wisconsin, and to the Jefferson Park area of Chicago. Later, others found their way west to Washington, Oregon, and California to grow vegetables and fruits, and establish vineyards. In Minnesota, Germans from Russia homesteaded farms and also worked at the St. Paul stockyards or contracted to work in the beet fields in Sibley and McLeod Counties until they had saved enough cash to buy acreage or start a business.

In 1978, Germans from Russia descendants in the Minneapolis/St Paul area established the North Star Chapter of Minnesota (Germans from Russia). For over 35 years, the North Star Chapter, whose membership is made up of descendants from many different areas in the United States and Russia, has provided educational programming on the topic of the Germans from Russia. With this book, we hope to share the stories of some of the descendants, reflecting on the legacy of the Germans from Russia in America.

There is a wealth of German-language literature about the Germans from Russia but the best comprehensive English-language books are:

Giesinger, Adam. *From Catherine to Khruschev: The Story of Russia's Germans*. Battleford, Saskatchewan, Canada: Marion Press, 1974.

Height, Joseph S. *Memories of the Black Sea Germans: Highlights of their History and* Heritage. Associated German-Russian Sponsors, 1979.

Schmidt, Ute. *Bessarabia, German Colonists on the Black Sea,* Germans from Russia Heritage Collection and Deutsches Kulturforum, 2011.

Stumpp, Karl. *The Emigration from Germany to Russia in the Years 1763 to 1862.* Lincoln, Nebraska: American Historical Society of Germans from Russia, 1982.

You may also visit the following websites to learn more about the culture of the Germans from Russia.

www.northstarchapter.org

library.ndsu.edu/grhc

cvgs.cu-portland.edu/origins.cfm

www.grhs.org

www.ahsgr.org

CHAPTER ONE

On the Land

Balzer Kleingartner farm, two miles north of Mercer, North Dakota.
The house and barn were built in 1919. The view is from the southeast
and shows wheat bundles put into shocks ready for the threshing crew
to arrive, August 1940. (Photo courtesy of Merv Rennich)

Hollyhocks

Sharon Chmielarz

Among the smells of hot tar
and newly mown lawn,
summer basks in intense
affairs with the garden's
biggest and boldest–
the peonies' mounds,
the yucca's white bells,
the northern hibiscus
called hollyhocks,
old-fashioned favorites
relegated to back rows,
to the south side of a shed,
to a yard's far corners,
to a white picket fence.
Petaled shells that
are havens for bees.
Voluminous leaves
wind shuffles and rumples.
The hollyhocks' kind
of old world. German
Russian humility calls
and calls
your name from the gate.

Picking Rock

Merv Rennich

He was standing up in the wagon yelling my name, "*Merf, gat dat von,*" pointing to a spot about twenty feet to the right of me. I tried to focus on what he was looking at, and I could not see anything. Of course, there were a lot of pebbles on the ground, but somehow he had seen one about the size of a golf ball, and he was determined that I pick it up. He kept directing me and repeating, "*Nein! Nein!, ofer der,*" and adding "*Gott im Himmel, was ist los mit du?*" until, almost on top of the little orb, I finally saw it and put it in my bucket. He was a persistent German Russian farmer.

I, along with three other friends, were picking rock off of summer fallow (crop land not planted for a season). The field had been cleared of rock before, but each year, for some reason, more rocks would appear. It was late June in central North Dakota and it was hot! Near a hundred degrees. We each had a bucket to collect the rocks and when the bucket was about full, or as full as we thought it should be, we would dump it into the farmer's wagon which, pulled by horses, slowly guided us down the field. When the amount of rocks in the wagon came to some predetermined level, the farmer would have the horses pull the wagon to a rock pile where we would unload it.

Occasionally we would come across a large rock that the spring thaw had brought partially to the surface. Since it would not fit into the bucket, it would have to be picked up by itself, sometimes using a shovel or a crow bar to dig it out, and carried to the wagon. It was back-breaking work, all for fifteen cents an hour. We started at seven a.m. and worked until one p.m. before the real heat of the afternoon set in.

Six hours of this would buy one pack of jumbo firecrackers with maybe a nickel or so left over. For some sparklers, roman candles, or a few cherry bombs, it was back to it the next day. How else could we afford to celebrate the Fourth of July?

4

Spring Planting

Andy Kroneberger

By the spring of 1944, my dad's health problems were getting worse. Our retired farmer who had planted the corn the previous year was not able to help due to his own ailments. I found myself on the two-row John Deere corn planter with a team of horses that was a half-bronco breed, even though I had never planted corn. I was fifteen, and in my sophomore year of high school. My German Volga-born dad, who immigrated to the United States in 1912, was able to acquaint me with the planter and got me started. After he watched me from the family car for several rounds, I was on my own.

Our family farm was in Nobles County near the town of Brewster, in southwestern Minnesota. My third day on the planter, I stopped in the middle of the field to remove a rock up ahead that was interfering with the planter's check wire. Fortunately, I had raised the planter out of the ground and had tied the driving lines securely to the planter's raising levers. As I removed the rock, the wire flipped and it snapped one of the horses on his leg. The team of horses took off like a bolt of lightning with the two-row planter hitched on behind them. I stood momentarily frozen in fright. They crossed the wire six times in the field before Fred Polzine, a neighbor who had witnessed the runaway, stopped his planting, tied his horses on his fence line, and came to my aid. He was able to catch the horses. Luckily, the planter's check wire had come loose from the planter and the damage to the eighteen hundred feet of planter wire was minimal. My father had watched the runaway from the farmyard and somehow found a way to get out to the field. The neighbor helped untangle the mess and soon the planter and horses were ready to go, but I was still shaken and said, no, I didn't want any more of this. My father swore at me in German, saying, "Dammit, get your butt on that planter and plant corn," and I did.

Later on in the afternoon the planting was going well and I was mentally back in the groove again, but my thoughts turned to my schooling. I wondered if any of my classmates ever had an experience as the one I just went through. After the corn was planted, I was able to return to school.

Excerpted from *A Man Called Andreas*: Kroneberger, Andy, 2010 pp. 136-7.

Team of horses on Karl Just farm, rural Zeeland, North Dakota.
Ephraim Just at right. (Photo courtesy of Carol Just)

Juneberries

James Gessele

One hundred years ago, turn-of-century German Russian immigrants settling on the Northern Great Plains—particularly in the upper half of North Dakota and the Canadian prairie provinces—observed a native fruit-bearing shrub called the Juneberry. To Canadians, the berry came to be known as the saskatoon, a corruption of the Cree Indian name *misaaskwatoomin*. Used as flavoring with dried meat in the preparation of pemmican, the Juneberry was long a food staple among Plains Indian tribes. Referred to as a berry, it is actually a pome fruit and goes by other names such as serviceberry, shadbush, and Rocky Mountain blueberry.

In June 1895, a North Dakota newspaper editor commented on the lush abundance of Juneberries along the Missouri River bottomlands: "It is known to the native Indians as the 'medicine berry' and is reckoned the best possible blood medicine when the ripe berry is eaten uncooked. It is almost impossible to harm oneself through gorging, and a two-week feast is liable to knock the doctor out of a good many fees."

Needing little to prompt innate resourcefulness, German Russian settlers soon made the sweet, blue-black, quarter-inch diameter fruit a part of their own diet. With buckets in tow, entire families headed for river and upland ravines the first days of July where the shrubs grew more prolific and the ripened fruit awaited picking.

Our family, too, was among those German Russian pickers, though my sister and I perceived it as drudgery and saw little value in it beyond what we stuffed in our mouths. Our mother launched into a lesson on that theme of resourcefulness and regaled us with a Great Depression/North Dakota drought-era story that had Grandpa facing feed shortages and certain ruin unless he fed his cattle Russian thistle. But he had to lace the thistle with surplus molasses provided to farmers by the federal government unless he was prepared to lose his cows to bloat. Grandma had an "aha" moment when preparing to can her Juneberries and realized she could substitute some of that molasses for sugar, which she couldn't afford anyway. If God gave us a gift, by golly, we had better make use of it.

Lesson learned, the picking ended and it was homeward bound. Once the fruit was washed and sorted, an array of culinary applications lay before our mother. Some folks used the harvest in making wine or preserves. Our mother set aside a portion for fresh baked sweets requiring fruit, such as the standard custard-laden *Kuchen*. The greater portion was dedicated to canning. During the ensuing winter months, jars of the delectable treat were pulled down from shelves and served as compote, drizzled with sweet cream and sprinkled with sugar. Sans syrup in mid-winter, the canned fruit was once again used in baking *Kuchen*.

Even today, successful harvesting is still apt to be found on northeast slopes where the bushes are less subject to spring frosts during the late April and early May bloom. Folklore says very early traders and pioneers observed the Juneberry blossoms as a signal that frost was sufficiently out of the ground for burial of the winter's dead, a case of resourcefulness to the bitter end.

Butchering Day
Bernelda Kallenberger Becker

Butchering day—the day set aside to put up meat for the coming winter. I hated it—the horrible smells, the steamy kitchen, and especially, some of the horseplay that accompanied the day. However the grown-ups, my uncle Edwin and aunt Christina, my grandfather Andreas, and my parents, seemed to think it great fun to work together.

Papa usually chose a chilly fall day. Mama made sure I stayed near the house until after the pigs met their demise. To keep me busy, she had me help carry water from the windmill in a gallon bucket. Butchering took lots of water. I helped Mama carry fruit jars from the damp cellar. The jars were dusty and the dead spiders in some of them frightened me. Mama would can some of the meat in the jars later. Aunt Christina washed the jars and put them into the boiling water in the copper boiler to sterilize them.

Grossfadder scraped and cut any morsel of edible material from the pig's head. Mama and my aunt cut the ears, heart, and kidneys into small cubes. All this was then stirred together and seasoned with salt and pepper while *Grossfadder* cleaned the stomach. Mama stuffed the cleaned stomach with this concoction. She then threaded a big needle with string she had saved from packages from the store, and sewed up the filled stomach. They boiled it in the copper boiler heating on Mama's Monarch kitchen range. Mama and I had spent the day before bringing corn cobs from the pig pen and *mischt* squares from behind the cow barn, storing them near the kitchen to use the next day to keep the range going full speed all day. Mama filled the sterilized pint jars with what had not fit into the stomach and processed them in the canner. In our German-speaking household, we called this *Schwartenmagen*. The kitchen became hot and steamy, filled with pleasant and unpleasant aromas.

Grossfadder's next job was to turn the intestines inside out and scrape them well so they could be used as casings for sausage. He sometimes asked me to hold one end down on the board while he scraped. Ugh! I felt more like holding my nose, but I helped him because I cherished time alone with him. He was usually too busy on the farm to pay attention to me.

After the pork chops, roasts, hams, and slabs of bacon had been set aside, Papa brought the remaining scraps of meat to the house to run through the grinder for sausage. Papa held the title of Champion Sausage Mixer and Seasoner in our family. He rolled up his sleeves and washed his hands. Then he stood at a washtub about two-thirds full of ground pork and began the process. I don't recall that he ever used a printed recipe. He would add a handful of salt, a bit of pepper, garlic my mother had chopped up, and sprinkle in some special seasoning he purchased at the butcher shop. Now and then he put some in his mouth for a taste test. When he decided it was about right, he asked the others to sample it too. They made a great production of this before it was seasoned to everyone's satisfaction.

The sausage stuffer machine fascinated me. They used it to fill the casings *Grossfadder* had prepared with the seasoned sausage. After about fourteen inches of casing were filled, our useful store string served the purpose of tying the ends to make one ring of sausage. Sometimes the adults would get silly and wrap the slimy sausages around each other's necks. I failed to see the fun in this and ran from the room before they did it to me. Sometimes I didn't run soon enough. It felt slimy and icky.

The next day, Papa hung the hams, bacon, and sausages in the smokehouse behind the granary. I don't remember how he made the smoke because he did it without me. But I remember going to the smokehouse afterwards to savor the smoky smell. Finally they hung the smoked meat on the rafters of the granary where they stayed all winter, providing many delicious meals.

Later that week, Mama put all the fatty scraps into a large kettle and rendered it for lard. She stored the lard in a large crock, interspersing layers of pre-fried meat and layers of lard, using the lard as a preservative. She then covered the crock and Papa carried it to the cellar. The cracklings that remained after rendering the lard were used in cookies and strudels. They joked that they used everything about the pig except the squeal.

Mama also used some of that lard to make lye soap to do her laundry—a somewhat dangerous process. I recall that one year the container she had the soap in to set leaked, and the lye ate a hole in the kitchen linoleum.

The unpleasant butchering day memories faded into the background when hunger pains rumbled in my stomach. Hungry when we returned from the weekly Saturday night shopping trip to town, we smacked our lips and relished the *Schwartenmagen* and a big slice of Mama's homemade bread. Waking up mornings to the smell of home-cured bacon sizzling in the pan started the day just right. The cookies Mama made with the lard, laced with the cracklings, were every bit as tasty as the Keebler's chocolate chip cookies my children clamored for. Mama's piecrusts were flakier than flaky, and her ham dinners were occasions for celebration.

These days I push a cart down the aisles of my local supermarket, purchase my groceries, and go on my leisurely way with seldom a thought to those days. But the sounds and smells of butchering days are stored deep in my memory's database. Sometimes I'm overtaken by nostalgia, and I long for those tastes and flavors of long ago. Then I remember the unpleasant smells, the work, and the inconveniences. Yes, I know. The food I purchase may not taste as good, but in return, I now have time and energy to enjoy a myriad of advantages my parents and grandparents never imagined. I'll *take* today, and *remember* yesterday.

Dockter Brothers: Kevin, Jeff, Tim, Joel, and Cameron pose
with the final product at their annual sausage making day,
February 2011. (Photo courtesy of Joel Dockter)

On The Farm

Elvera Hepner Hofmann

The summer days are hot and long
While the birds still sing their song.
The straws of wheat dry in the sun
While grasshoppers jump on the run.

The cows are lying down to rest
While the calves are put to the test.
Cavorting about like only they can
Growing, hoping to stay away from man.

The pigs are rolling in the grass
While the little ones snuggle in a mass.
Winter will come and who will it be
To fill the larder for all to see.

The garden is bountiful row by row
While rains would help what we sow.
The vegetables are still mostly green
With specks of color in between.

The horses are swatting the flies
While clouds above fill the skies.
No harness, no work today
Just graze and graze away.

Waldemar Kremer photograph, with permission.

CHAPTER TWO

Heimweh

(Homesickness)

(Waldemar Kremer photograph, with permission)

Song of the Meadowlark

Dallas D. Zimmerman

From a land called Russia the Germans came,
A hundred years ago;
To settle a new land was their aim,
Across the sea so wide;
To homestead the prairies of Mid-America
Where the grass grew long,
And the meadowlark vibrantly sang his song.

They broke the sod of a new land,
But kept the ways of the old;
Traditions–centuries old–they kept in hand
In grassy islands of culture;
They labored hard, prayed, and sometimes played,

In the Old German way,
And the larks of the meadows echoed their song.

Now we–their children and grandchildren–have migrated anew,
Away from the prairies;
Away to settle in places where "Our People" are few,
And the cultures many;
To cities of concrete walls and manicured lawns
Where the All-American robin is king,
And the meadowlark is seldom heard to sing.

How oft we yearn to return to the prairie fold,
Our few remaining kin;
To witness again that song of old,
The traditions of the settlers;
But whence we return we with sadness hear
A much weaker song;
A song more distant, less clear,
Ever competing and blending with modern tunes.
And we lament over what the prairie has lost.

But should we stop on the prairie
At dusk,
And inwardly reflect
We may with greater sadness find
That the song within us
Is weaker too;
Less clear,
Changed from the days of our youth,
And changing still.
May we not stop

And silently pray

That the song

Will not

Fade

Away.

May the larks of the meadows sing on and on.

Previously published in the North Star Chapter of Minnesota Newsletter, Volume 11, Number 3, April 1987.

Work Day at the Country School

Bernelda Kallenberger Becker

In 1934, one-room schools on the South Dakota prairie hadn't heard of kindergarten. Since my birthday fell in February, I couldn't enter first grade until the coming fall. At six and one-half years of age, I had been ready and waiting to start school for eons.

One day in late August, after the morning milking had been completed, my Papa hitched Schimmel and Schwarz to a wagon. I watched him load it with items such as a spade, hammer, pliers, a cream can filled with water, and sundry other tools and equipment. Mama brought a broom and a box filled with rags, furniture polish, and a scrub brush from the house and placed them in the wagon. Finally, she brought a box filled with freshly baked *Kuchen*, a loaf of homemade bread, slices of home-cured ham, and molasses cookies. The day had been set aside to clean and polish the schoolhouse for the coming school year. I eagerly climbed up into the wagon. The horses plodded along. Anxious to get there, I wished I dared to take the reins from Papa's hands and crack them over the horses' rumps to make them hurry. Tiring of my unending questions and bouncing on the wagon seat, Mama made me sit behind her on the floor of the wagon box.

When we entered the schoolyard, I immediately recognized uncles and aunts, cousins, and neighbors, some standing round visiting in their *Schwäbisch* language, the language used throughout our Germans from Russia community, and some already at work. I handed Aunt Christina the broom Mama had given me to bring inside. Having no older siblings, I had never been inside the schoolhouse. I stood, just inside the door, and looked around in awe. Large and small desks were strategically placed around a pot-bellied heater standing in the center of the rectangular room. At the front of the room stood a larger desk, an American flag in a stand stood beside it. I pondered who the men in the pictures on the wall might be. Surely they were important to be there. Shelves behind glass doors drew me toward them like a magnet. They were filled with books. The only book at our house was a Bible. I had longed for books since forever. Mama had told me I would learn to read when I attended school. I turned away with regret when my cousin Elaine urged me to come outside to play.

We younger children spent the day amusing ourselves by locating gopher holes in the schoolyard, playing London Bridge or Drop the Handkerchief, and running in and out of the building asking questions of men and women, making a general nuisance of ourselves.

Everyone else worked. Dressed in their best housedresses, our mothers washed windows, desks, and the gray wooden floor. Older girls dusted books and the teacher's desk, washed the blackboard, and cleaned chalk erasers by taking them outside and clapping them together.

Fathers and the older boys took turns manually digging two deep, rectangular holes. With lots of grunts and groans, they moved the two outhouses over them. The smelly holes where they had been were filled with dirt that had been removed digging the new holes. Someone had furnished last year's Montgomery Ward and Sears Roebuck catalogs to supply bathroom tissue for the coming year.

At midday, Mrs. Kurle, my cousin Thelma's mother, appeared at the schoolhouse door and rang a bell she held in her hand. My cousin Alice told us this was the signal to come in for dinner. That is what we called our noon meal. By this time I had learned that the large desk belonged to the teacher. The ladies had covered it with the good food they had brought: slices of fresh bread, chokecherry and plum jelly, sliced tomatoes, cucumber salad, slices of sausage and ham, several kinds of cookies, pies, and Mama's prune *Kuchen*. She made it best, I thought. My eyes quickly scanned the array of desserts. Had anyone furnished an angel food cake? Mama didn't make it because it took too many eggs. She saved her eggs to sell when we went to town on Saturday nights. I saw just one cake, standing tall and regal, and it even had frosting! Fearful that it would all be gone before I'd get a piece, I hurriedly filled my plate under Mama's watchful eye, and ate as fast as I could so I could get back to pick up my dessert. Rules in our German Russian community were rigid. First you ate sensible food. Only then could you have dessert— and even then, only one dessert. The grown-ups joked and visited while they ate, filling the room with a wonderful spirit of *Gemütlichkeit*.

Dinner finished, everyone returned to his or her task. My uncle Edwin's Model A Ford truck chugged into the schoolyard and backed up to a cellar window. Several men helped him shovel his load of lignite coal into the cellar. I knew the hungry potbellied stove in the schoolroom would devour it during the coming winter.

I had heard my parents say that the Miller and Roemmich children lived too far from school to walk. They came in wagons driven by older brothers. I understood immediately why their fathers unloaded fresh hay into the barn. I already knew there would be mornings when my cousin, Floyd, would also drive a wagon if it was raining or below zero. I looked forward to such a morning when my cousins, Waldon and Elaine, would snuggle with me in fresh straw, wrapped in blankets.

I ran inside to tell Mama what I'd seen. She had just placed a new white enamel bucket and dipper on a table at the back of the room. I had been with her when she had purchased it at the Eureka Bazaar on a recent Saturday night.

"Where will the water come from to fill it?" I asked. "There's no well here at the school."

"The teacher brings it in a cream can and keeps the bucket full," she told me.

Next to the water bucket stood a tin basin to wash hands. Aunt Christina hung a clean towel on a nail above the basin and laid several more on a shelf above the table.

The sun was dropping in the western sky and some of the families had already left. But several had stayed, along with my parents, to varnish the desks. Mama told me they did this last so there would be no dust in the air while the new finish dried. I breathed deep, enjoying the aroma of the wet lacquer and wondered which would be my desk. One of the older Miller girls had told me beginners sat at the front. The golden glow of sunlight streaming through the one western window promised exciting days to come.

Mama closed the door one final time just as Papa drove up. *"Mach's schnell,"* he called from the wagon seat. "I've got cows to milk." Mama lifted me into the wagon. Worn out from the day's excitement, I had no memory of reaching home.

Crown Molding

Nancy Gertner

"Would you like crown molding with that?" asked Harold as we reviewed my order for materials needed to replace the roof on the 1899 schoolhouse on the Minnesota prairie.

"Yes, of course," I replied. The Shady Nook School, operated as District 48 (county) and later as District 358 (state), closed in 1966. The roof had sprung a few leaks over the years, and the time to restore was imminent. Using Economics 101 learned from my father, I ordered locally, from the nearest lumber supplier. During restoration, the old doorframe revealed that Westbrook Lumber Company also served as the supplier for the lumber and materials used to modify and maintain the building during its sixty-seven years of operation. Now called Westbrook Home Center, the manager, Harold Lamb, is a brother of my high school classmate and friend April Lamb. Harold made site visits to measure the building for materials and delivered the supplies.

The school was built in the North Prairie School style, with a wooden clapboard exterior, a vestibule, and a steeply pitched roof with a brick chimney. An early spring tornado in 1998 blew the bell tower off the roof. The five-panel wooden schoolhouse door had weathered enough to permit raccoons to inhabit the school.

This prairie school educated three generations of new Americans. For my grandfather, Herman Gärtner, school gave him an anglicized name, making him Herman Gertner, while his parents remained Gärtners. Grandfather and the other students received fifteen minutes of daily instruction in the native language of their parents: German.

Early school records show that German was taught in the school in the early 1900s. The children on the south side of the nearest town, Westbrook, were mainly born to German immigrant families, and the families on the north side of town were descended mostly from Norwegian and Scandinavian immigrants. Located less than two miles from the Murray County border, the school is located in the western part of Cottonwood County, about twenty miles from the town of Mountain Lake, where the Mennonite Germans from South Russia settled beginning around 1874. About a dozen Lutheran families from the Grunau District of South Russia settled in western Cottonwood County, in Rosehill Township.

As the families grew and wanted more farms, they spread westward into Murray County and south into Nobles County. In the 1880s, several families of Galician Mennonites arrived from the Austrian Empire and built their own Mennonite church and cemetery in Rosehill Township. These Mennonites apparently spoke the same German dialect as the Germans from Russia, *Plattdeutsch*, and marriages between the families were frequent. The Lutherans also built a church and cemetery in Rosehill Township in the 1880s. The Mennonites closed their country church around 1950, and the Lutherans closed theirs in 1974. The cemeteries remain operational. My mother decorated the family graves on Memorial Day weekend. After her passing, my sister and I carry on this tradition.

The March morning in 2012 was very foggy as I drove slowly over the hill, looking for the first glimpse of my schoolhouse that had withstood yet another winter on the prairie. There she stood, workers patching holes in the wooden roof after the cedar shake shingles were removed, apparently the original shingles from the 1899 construction. Plywood sheathing was added as underlayment for the new shingles. I stood under the Colorado blue spruce tree, planted, I believe, during the 1940s by Mrs. Kleve and her students. I painted the crown molding white.

The contracted work crew did the skilled construction work. Recommended by the materials supplier, the contractor also had a school connection to my family. Kim Miller's wife, Debbie Oleson, was a former first grader of my mother, Flossie Mitchell Gertner. I worked on the opposite side of the contractors, trying to keep out of their way, as I prepared and painted the weathered siding. When they ate lunch, I borrowed their platform scissor lift to reach the high places. They listened to country music on the radio and used noisy power tools. On days when they were doing farm work, and I worked alone, my company was birds and their songs, and an occasional critter, like a mouse or a woodchuck. Looking across the road, I could see the resting place of my great-great-grandmother Katharina Deutschmann Hochbaum's younger sister Elisabeth Siemund, who died before the Rosehill Emmanuel Cemetery was established. This Deutschmann sister who married Mr. Siemund apparently died in childbirth, trying to deliver one of the first babies in Rosehill Township. A patch of prairie grass that farmers have skirted around for over one hundred and thirty years marks her grave.

The ambitious contractor offered to rebuild the school's east wall, which had sliding doors for the machine shed the retired schoolhouse had become. After laying concrete footings, the wall was erected. At Harold's office at the Westbrook Home Center, I selected the windows for the new wall. The made-in-Minnesota Marvin Windows are a "true divided light" style that matches the original windows quite closely.

Giving the crown molding a second coat of paint along the roofline gave me a bird's eye view of the farmland. The warm early spring of 2012 enabled early fieldwork, and I listened and watched as the farmers planted soybeans and corn in their fields adjacent to the school. The crops grew, and the hay in the road ditches was cut, raked, and baled. The schoolhouse gradually took on the whiteness of primer paint. The school was originally painted white, but had taken on a new life as a red school during its years as a machine shed. I deliberated on the paint color, and decided to stay with red. Since its 1899 construction in the horse and buggy days, the traffic on the road close to the school building includes cars and trucks that speed by and stir up a great deal of dust. I decided the red color would match the gravel dust better than white paint.

The hours of painting alone provided time to reflect on my five years of schooling in this one room school in the 1960s. I don't remember it feeling cold, though there was no insulation in the walls. How different it was from the twenty-first century classroom. No computers. We had textbooks, maps, and a globe. We had flashcards, and the Palmer alphabet displayed above the chalkboard. We had *Weekly Reader* on Fridays and chocolate milk. The school had electricity and a refrigerator that held our milk in glass bottles with foil tops. The 1957 addition provided indoor plumbing. We drank the well water from faucets in the restrooms, which were not heated since the furnace sat in the middle of the schoolroom and did not have ducting. However, having indoor plumbing was better than going outdoors to the vintage outhouses that still sat on their foundations.

I also recalled the first time I painted the schoolhouse, as a teenager. Five years after the school was closed and my mother bought it at auction, my family changed the building's color from white to red. I spent many days during my sixteenth summer scraping the building and preparing it for painting. The actual painting was done one weekend, with my older sisters home from their school and work, and our parents helping as well. Dad positioned the tractor with the scoop bucket and the grain elevator to help me reach the high spots. Mom stayed close to the ground, a fact I appreciate as I realized she was the same age then as I am now. The second family school painting event was twenty years later, five years after Dad had died. Mother was in her late 70s, and my sister Joan brought along her eight-year-old daughter, Sarah. Following the passing of our parents, I became the owner of the school and two and a half acres of land. The school was overdue for painting, as it had been twenty-one years since the last painting.

In early July, preparations were complete for the 2012 school reunion and painting party. The tall grass in the schoolyard was mowed. Two portable privies were delivered. My cousin Marlo Lindstrom and my husband, Paul Maggitti, helped me set up wooden picnic tables on a beastly hot day.

The picnic day was a beautiful twenty-five degrees cooler than the rest of the week, and suitable for painting and being outdoors. If I build it, will they come? Yes! People came to paint, and to picnic. Former students with children and grandchildren attended the picnic and painting party. The only living schoolteacher, Dolores Ewy Gertner, came from Winona, Minnesota. The septuagenarians proved to be the superstars, with Dennis Lidtke bringing ladders and his tractor with the bucket scoop to reach up high, and his wife, Mary, painting the high gable on the south end with my cousin Leonard Mitchell, and my cousin Marlo Lindstrom up on the ladder on the east side. Dianne Lidtke Legler painted on the south side, and my cousin Jan Mitchell registered the guests and gave students a gold star for each year of school.

At three p.m., it was time to break for the picnic, so we ceased painting and ate our potluck picnic and enjoyed some visit time. A few sprinkles of rain prompted people to pack and leave as the schoolhouse stood bright barn red against the prairie sky. What was left unpainted would wait for another paint day.

I had several more solitary paint days in 2012. One day while I painted, farmer Terry Appel harvested the eighty acres of soybeans across the road. I watched the bean dust settle into my wet paint as he emptied his combine's grain into the truck. My last workday was Columbus Day. I felt like I had rediscovered a little bit of America on the Minnesota prairie.

Shady Nook School has survived her one hundred and thirteen prairie winter. When the weather is warm enough, I will get out my paint and brushes, and return to the prairie. I hope my aging knees will still be able to climb the ladder.

Shady Nook School, Rosehill Township, Cottonwood County, Minnesota, 2013. (Photo courtesy of Nancy Gertner)

Leaving a Mark

Dallas D. Zimmerman

As a youngster growing up on the Dakota prairie there was often time to stop and wonder about marks left on the land by those who had passed before. The wallows left by the buffalo brought forth mental pictures of large beasts rolling in clouds of dust. Rolling perhaps for pleasure or perhaps for necessity to ward off pestering flies. The "Indian Rings," marks left on the hilltops by wandering tribes, triggered the imagination. Although we were taught in school that the circles of stones were placed to keep the cold Dakota winds out of the buffalo-skin tents, it was more exciting to imagine red-faced men dancing around the circles at dusk.

Last summer I had an opportunity to return to the prairie and the "Old Place," my farm home of some thirty years ago. The road was muddy from a recent rain as I drove to the farm to look around. To my surprise I found the old marks on the prairie less clear now. The buffalo wallows having been leveled considerably with the passing years. The "Indian Ring" on the hill west of the old farm site was hardly visible, having almost been swallowed up by the sod. It took some imagination to close the circle.

Very little remains of the "Old Place." All that is left of the home is the basement, now just a hole in the ground filled with trash. The old barn built by my German Russian great-grandfather Dalke collapsed many years ago, and much of the wood has rotted away. Only a rhubarb plant still growing in the old garden and the windmill squeaking in the wind seemed like real monuments of my boyhood days.

But then as I was about to leave I noticed something that I had almost forgotten, a plateau in the hillside by the house. The place where the new barn was to be located. A new barn had been a dream of my father's for more years than I can remember. A site, a shelf in the hillside, was to be prepared. A lot of earth had to be moved; the hill lowered. So it was that Father would from time to time hitch the scoop to the tractor and move some earth. It was never clear whether he undertook the earth-moving whenever he felt happy and optimistic about the future or did it when he was depressed and needed this work to boost his spirits.

The work that Father had done was not always appreciated. Removal of the sod and top soil had exposed clay that clung tenaciously to your shoes when you walked through the area after a rain. It didn't seem like he had made much progress in all the years of preparing the site. It seemed like a lot of work remained to be done. Now twenty-five years after his death, the site oddly looked ready to accept the barn. The grass had grown up and stabilized the soil. The impression he left was much more visible now. The mark representing a lot of hard work and hope was more apparent to me now than ever.

With some sadness I left the farm and drove back over the muddy road leading to the highway. As I closed the gate I looked back and wondered whether anyone would notice my tracks before they were washed away by the next rain.

Previously published in the North Star Chapter of Minnesota Newsletter, Volume 12, Number 4, November 1988.

Old farm house on the prairie
(Craig Martin Stellmacher photograph, with permission)

A Holiday Memory

Chris Huber

The favorite memory I have of Christmas past is from my childhood. As a child of immigrant South Dakota farming parents, the Depression of the 1930s remains a most vivid memory for me. Even though our family was extremely poor in material things, we had wonderful community and church get-together events and activities.

A yearly high point for me was our country church's annual children's Christmas program. St. John's Lutheran Church, rural Hosmer, South Dakota, was still conducted in the German language and tradition and therefore the children's program consisting of children reciting German religious Christmas poems and stories individually and collectively as well as singing many German Christmas religious folk songs.

Program practices took place at the church and began in early November. Every Wednesday evening, my parents would pack us, their six children, into the unheated Ford Model A sedan and off to practice we would go. After many weeks of practice, the big night arrived.

The country church would be filled, the kerosene lamp chandeliers would be illuminated, the pot-bellied stove would be glowing red from overheating, and the children would be seated in the front pews–the girls on the left side of the aisle in the women's section and the boys on the right side of the aisle in the men's section.

After all were seated, the ushers would come forward and light the hundreds of wax candles on the decorated Christmas tree (the ushers and their water pails would remain next to the tree during the entire program just in case one of the flickering candles would ignite the tree). The audience was hushed and the program began. The other children and I proudly recited our memorized pieces and loudly sang our songs.

Once the program concluded, bags of treats were given to each child. The bags contained glorious treasure–hard ribbon candy, boxes of animal crackers, homemade marble fudge and cookies as well as nuts of all descriptions plus a large, delicious apple or orange.

The tree candles were then individually extinguished and in the warm flickering glow of the chandelier lamps, all would sing "*Stille Nacht, Heilige Nacht.*"

As we were bundled into the warm comforter in the back seat of the unheated Model A and drove homeward, the excitement of the evening and satisfaction of participating with my cousins, neighbors, and friends truly has made this one of my most joyous holiday memories.

Previously published in the *Fridley Focus*, Fridley, Minnesota.

Midnight Mass at St. Mary's Catholic Church, Ellis, Kansas

Rosemary Wiesner Larson

The children from the lower grades of St. Mary's School assembled in the schoolhouse next to the church about an hour before the solemn High Mass began. There was a flurry of activity to find the white angel gown that fit best. Then the procession from the school to the church through the cold, crisp air, moving rapidly into the back of the church.

About fifteen minutes before midnight, the little angels walked down the center aisle, their gold tinsel halos sparkled in the bright lights, as they sang "O Little Town of Bethlehem" until the children reached the crèche in front of the right side altar.

Standing in front of the manger, they sang all three verses of "Silent Night" in German, a song they'd rehearsed many times to learn all the words:

> *Stille Nacht, Heilige Nacht,*
> *Alles schläft, einsam wacht*
> *Nur das traute hochheilige Paar,*
> *Holder Knabe im lockigen Haar,*
> *Schlaf in himmlischer Ruh!*
> *Schlaf in himmlischer Ruh!*

At midnight the huge pipe organ that seemed to reach to the sky burst forth in the solemn music of a Latin High Mass. The organ was played by Leo Wiesner, who was the St. Mary's organist for twenty-six years, beginning in 1922. During Midnight Mass, Leo was accompanied by his children: three played their violins; one, the clarinet; and another, the saxophone.

The beautiful voices of the choir and the accompanying instrumental music were a most fitting tribute to God on the night that the birth of

Jesus Christ is celebrated. "*Adeste Fidelis*" and "Hark the Herald Angels Sing" were interspersed with the sung prayers of the Latin Mass: the Kyrie, the Credo, the Gloria, the Pater Noster, and the Agnus Dei.

Indeed, Midnight Mass at St. Mary's Catholic Church was always a memorable event in those early years. Many came from miles around to attend Midnight Mass in Ellis, Kansas, to hear the talented Wiesner family play.

These are my fond memories of growing up in the 1930s. Yes, I was one of the angels.

St. Mary's Catholic Church, Ellis, Kansas.
(Photo courtesy of Rosemary Wiesner Larson)

Kuchen: What's in It for Me?

James Gessele

True to form, *Kuchen* was served at every afternoon break during the 2003 Germans from Russia Heritage Society national convention in Rapid City, South Dakota. As in past events, it was a given feature of the gathering. After all, the South Dakota state legislature decreed this cholesterol bomb the state dessert.

It was available by the piece for a nominal donation. Whole ones went for five dollars. I bought a whole one to keep me company on the long drive through God's country on the return trip to North Dakota. My favorites, rhubarb and prune, were already sold out so I settled for peach.

By the time I reached Belfield, North Dakota, three-fourths of my distraction had vanished—in part out of hunger, in measure out of concern for the egg ingredients spoiling on me. I was on a mission to eat the whole thing and needed a cup of coffee to wash down the remainder. So I took a break at the deli section of the first available gas station. An icy glare was directed at me and my piece of peach when I paid for just one coffee and had the temerity to sit in one of their booths. It was then that my tackiness struck me. It was akin to Grandma taking her kids to a restaurant on a once-in-a-lifetime shopping trip to Bismarck back in the 1920s, breaking out a lunch she had packed for the gang, and then only ordering a glass of water for each one of her brood.

As I sat and contemplated how many hens suffered untold agony in laying the eggs for this wondrous German Russian concoction, I noticed the nutrition facts label on the wrapper. And here, after enough digression, we finally get to my point: How nutritious is *Kuchen* anyway? Well, this is what was on the label:

NUTRITION FACTS

Serving Size 1/6 *Kuchen* (2.7 oz/76g)
Servings Per Container About 6

Amount Per Serving:
Calories 180
Calories from Fat 45

% Daily Volume

Total Fat 6.0g	9%
Saturated Fat 2.0g	10%
Cholesterol 55mg	18%
Sodium 220mg	9%
Total Carbohydrates 28g	9%
Dietary Fiber 1g	4%
Sugars 11g	
Protein 4g	
Vitamin A 2% · Vitamin C 0%	
Calcium 2% · Iron 4%	

The remainder of nutrition labels I never have understood, so we can skip that part. But the list of ingredients grabbed my attention. Get a load of this:

INGREDIENTS: Enriched wheat flour bleached (malted barley flour, iron, niacin, thiamine, mononitrate, riboflavin, folic acid), water, soybean oil, yeast, whole eggs, sugar, contains 2% or less of: whey powder, sodium aluminum phosphate, sodium bicarbonate, salt, L-cysteine, monohydrochloride, dextrose, soy flour, diacetyl tartaric acid, esters of monodiglycerides, (DATEM), lecithin, vegetable powder, ascorbic acid, wheat starch, carbamide, calcium phosphate, fungal enzymes, sodium stearoyl lactolate, natural and artificial flavor, corn starch, turmeric, red cartenal FILLING ALSO INCLUDES: cream, modified corn starch, non-fat milk solids, sliced peaches, propylene glycol.

So, let us consider this. Is it worth one's good health to even contemplate a slice? Reading that litany of weird ingredients and digesting the calorie count both literally and figuratively in Belfield, on Sunday, September 7, 2003, I felt like a pig. But in spite of that, and to the everlasting credit of Lapp's Bakery in Hebron, North Dakota, this *Kuchen* tasted darn good. At least as good as Mom's or Grandma's.

As Grandma Lydia rolled out the dough before her little grandson whose nose barely cleared the table-top, you don't suppose she meant that list of alien ingredients when she sighed "...*und dann noch etwas Liebe dazu* (... and add a measure of love").

Custard kuchen fresh out of the oven.
(Photo courtesy of Carol Just)

CHAPTER THREE

Was Sprichst Du?

(What Do You Speak?)

Teacher Eugene Werre with first grade class,
Rosenthal School Distr. No. 3, McPherson County, South Dakota, 1934.
(Photo courtesy of Bernelda Kallenberger Becker)

The Bogeyman in My Closet
Bernelda Kallenberger Becker

Fear dampened my eager anticipation of the first day of school. What if I couldn't understand the teacher? My cousin Floyd, entering sixth grade, had told me that Mr. Werre taught classes using English. "*Vas isch das* English, Floyd?" I asked. Floyd spoke some words I couldn't understand. "*Das isch* English," he said. "It's the language in America."

Our German grandparents had immigrated to America from South Russia. We spoke *Schwäbisch* at our house. All of our relatives and neighbors did, too. How could I ever get my tongue around such strange sounds? Jumbled up dreams about it disturbed my restless nights.

Every morning I asked the same question. "*Mama, kann ich heit Morge' zur Schule geh?*" "Not this morning, Tootsie," she would say. "Be patient."

We had purchased a new tablet with a pretty picture of Mickey Mouse on the cover, two new pencils, an eraser, and a new box of eight crayons. I would spread them out on the kitchen table to admire. Mama understood my overwhelming temptation to draw on the tablet paper with the crayons. "Put them away, Tootsie," she'd say. "You want to have them nice and new when you go to school." I despaired that the day would ever come.

Finally, one night when Mama tucked me into bed, she said, "*Morgan ist der Tag.* You'll have to rise early to get dressed for school." Before I closed my eyes and tried to fall asleep, I folded my hands, and sent an urgent plea toward heaven, "*Jesu, helfen mir mit das englisch.*" English lurked in my fearful mind like the bogeyman in my closet.

The next morning Mama laid my new school clothes on the bed. I liked my pretty new red and white checked shirt, but I balked at the bib overalls and boy's high-topped shoes. "Can't I please wear my church-going dress and patent leather shoes," I begged. "They are for special days," Mama said. "But today is special," I whined. "All the girls will wear clothes like this, Tootsie," Mama said. "They are best for the long walk to school." Ready to throw a tantrum, one look at her tightly closed lips warned me the subject was closed. I dressed as fast as I could because I wanted to be ready when my cousins stopped by to take me with them. The legs of the stiff new overalls went swish, swish, swish as I walked to the kitchen.

"Tootsie, bring me that new, clean syrup pail. I have to pack your lunch." I ran and brought it from the pantry, jumping up and down with excitement as Mama spread fresh homemade bread with butter and a thick slice of liverwurst. She wrapped it in wax paper she had saved from a corn flakes box. For dessert she added a *plachinda*, my favorite pumpkin turnover. Finally, she filled a small mayonnaise jar with milk she had cooled in the cellar. My school supplies were already in a brown paper bag.

I sat down to my bowl of oatmeal and milk, but kept running to the window to watch for my neighbor cousins: Floyd, entering sixth grade; Waldon, entering fourth grade; and Elaine, also starting first grade. I'd barely finished eating when they arrived. I checked out Elaine's clothes. What a relief—they were almost identical to mine. The four of us followed a wagon trail across the pasture and over the rolling hills. They each carried a half-gallon syrup pail, too. Buoyed up by my excitement, I scarcely noticed the mile-long walk. When the school came into view I quickly scanned the girls playing in the schoolyard. Not one wore a dress.

Floyd showed Elaine and me the shelf in the cloakroom where we stored our syrup pails. Then he led us back outside to play. Mr. Werre came outside and raised the American flag to the top of the flagpole. A short while after that he came to the door and gave several shakes to the bell. Elaine and I ran to Floyd and placed our hands in his. His warm clasp helped calm my fears. He knew what to do. I could depend on Floyd to guide me through this first morning in the first grade. Even though filled with trepidation about this new thing called English, I determined I would conquer it.

The door closed behind us. The first day of school had begun!

Clouds Filled with Dust and Grasshoppers, Plus a God Who Speaks German

Hertha Bieber Lutz

My ancestors came from villages about forty miles apart in the German-settled area northwest of Odessa in South Russia, the Buechlers from Neu Glückstal, and the Biebers from Glückstal.

Yes, that's Bieber as in Justin Bieber. My teenage granddaughter, Katie, has an iron bedstead that I received from my grandmother Frederika Bieber. When I told Katie she's the fifth Bieber generation sleeping in it, she screamed, "Oh, are we related to Justin Bieber!" I said I didn't know, but Katie's peers are now hearing it's most certainly true.

I was born in 1929 on a farm a few miles east of Hosmer, South Dakota. My mother, Marie Buechler, was born in 1900 into a family that had emigrated in 1890, just a year after South Dakota became a state. They settled northwest of Bowdle, about a dozen miles west of where the Biebers would land.

My dad, Christian Bieber, was born in 1897, and in 1907 emigrated from Glückstal as a ten-year-old with his family to the Hosmer area. My grandfather Philip Bieber had been conscripted into the Russian military in the 1880s. He said he moved his family from South Russia to the Dakota prairie so his sons would not have to serve in the Czar's army.

Guess what! Ten years later my dad was drafted into the United States Army, and prepared to fight in World War I. The war ended before he was sent to Europe, but Christian Bieber always said being drafted here was okay, even if it meant fighting Germans. Why? Because the Biebers identified fully as citizens of their new nation, which they'd never done in Russia.

Memories from my early childhood are dominated by awareness of how difficult farming was in the mid-30s. Year after year, a dreadful lack of rain resulted in dust storms. We truly were dirt-poor. Then came the invasion by dark clouds, bringing not rain but hordes of grasshoppers. They came several summers and consumed much of whatever grain we were able to grow.

**Hertha Bieber Lutz, age ten, with her grandmother,
Fredericka Huber Bieber, age seventy-five, in front of the
farmhouse east of Hosmer, South Dakota, 1939.
(Photo courtesy of Hertha Bieber Lutz)**

We had no indoor plumbing and our only electricity, via a small, roof-mounted wind charger, powered one light in our kitchen and a radio. The absence of power and running water was not unique to Germans from Russia but was standard in rural parts of the Dakotas until around mid-20th century.

The memories that are most fascinating for me today have to do with language. My first language was German, as was true for all of my kin and for most everyone living in communities of north-central South Dakota. Learning English began for me when I entered first grade. All of my public-school education, eight grades in a one-room country school and four years of high school in the town of Hosmer, was in English.

Not so with my religious education. Worship and Sunday School at my congregation, St. John Lutheran in Hosmer, was in German consistently through nearly all of my first eighteen years. I studied Luther's *Small Catechism* in its original language and was confirmed in German, right in the middle of World War II.

I later learned that Lutherans of German background elsewhere in the Midwest stopped using German at church in those years because of anti-German hysteria. Where I lived everybody was German, so using an "enemy's" language never became an issue.

I recall that shortly after the war ended, my congregation began offering worship in English on some occasions. I had an uncle who refused to attend such services. He said, "God's language is German. Want proof? Hear God speaking to Adam in the Garden of Eden." Then he quoted from Genesis 3:9, "*Adam, wo bist du?*" Uncle John wasn't kidding; he really believed the Bible's original language was German.

As I discovered years later, the German of my youth was far from the classical *Hochdeutsch* that's written and spoken by most Germans today. We spoke a low German dialect that my ancestors brought with them from Russia.

My chief assessment of growing up a young German from Russia in South Dakota during the 1930s and 1940s, the first eighteen years of my life, is that I felt I was entirely normal. We were a completely homogeneous community. All the people I knew shared the same heritage. We knew there were some others called "Indians," but they lived quite far away.

I didn't know there was anything distinctive about growing up German from Russia until I left home for college and the larger world. Only then was I able to see that I was part of a unique human family. Neither superior nor inferior, but different—and special in ways I still savor.

My dear Creator God, thanks be to you—*Danke schön, mein Gott*—whatever language you're now hearing.

That Pioneering Spirit

Nancy Gertner

I grew up on the family farm in southwestern Minnesota with two farm-raised parents that also grew up in Rosehill Township of Cottonwood County. "Where's your pioneering spirit?" was a phrase my two older sisters and I frequently heard from our mother, who was a school teacher with a twenty-nine-year career in public education in addition to being a farm wife. This was perhaps most frequently used when her daughters were reluctant to do something that she thought needed to be done.

The farm girls in my family helped on the farm by picking rocks, "walking beans" and pulling the weeds, and helped tend the animals, including chicken, sheep, swine, cattle, and horses. I was amused to learn my immigrant great-great-grandparents had first gone to Kansas in 1875, and moved north to Minnesota, thinking the Kansas soil was too rocky. Every spring, the Minnesota soil "hatched" new baby rocks that were hazardous to the farm equipment that planted and harvested the crops. My father never gave up his Belgian draft horses, using them to mow the steep road ditches since they would not tip over like a tractor. Dad also used the horses to plant corn, thinking he could get the rows straighter than with the tractor, and I remember riding on the planter with him when I was a preschooler.

"What does one man need four tractors for?" my mother, Flossie Mitchell Gertner, would ask about my father's farm equipment. My dad, Leo Gertner, was very proud of his John Deere tractor, which he purchased new in 1938. My sisters, Joan and Marcia, and I learned to drive that tractor, with a hand clutch, but Dad always had to start it for us since it had a flywheel starter. We learned how to drive on the small Ford tractor, which was purchased after WWII, along with an Oliver and a Farmall. Each tractor had its specific uses, such as cultivating, combining, disking, plowing, hauling wagons, or running the grain elevator. The Farmall had a front-end scoop loader.

In the 1960s, Dad purchased an Oliver tractor with a cab, and got a snow blower for this tractor. The early cabs had no luxury features like heaters, air conditioning, or radio.

While my grandmothers, Sophia Yahnke Gertner and Martha Mischke Mitchell, did not have easy lives on their farms in Rosehill Township, they saw the addition of electricity and telephones in the 1940s, and had homes heated with furnaces to keep them warm in the winter. They had wood-fired cook stoves and large gardens. They canned food to keep their families self-sufficient, along with the farm-raised animals that were used for meat.

My great-grandmothers, Elisabeth Hochbaum Gärtner and Julia Grams Jahnke, had difficult lives and were very isolated from other women and families, living on their homesteads that were typically a half-mile or more from the next closest farm. My great-grandmother Gärtner was a young wife who gave birth to ten babies on the Minnesota prairie.

Great-great-grandmother Hochbaum was a middle-aged woman when she immigrated with her husband and children. Her sister-in-law Regina Zöller Deutschmann was widowed just days after her husband had filed his homestead claim, and she worked the farm with the help of her children, and proved up on the homestead claim seven years after her husband died. What a hard life she must have had, and I suspect she may have regretted that decision to leave behind their life on the steppe of South Russia, where the families lived in villages with tree-lined streets, and the children had neighbors to play with, and the women had companionship nearby.

My pioneer ancestors left me no diaries or memoirs, so my insight into their lives is derived from looking at homestead claims on file at the National Archives and Records Administration (NARA) in Washington, DC.

Minnesota celebrated a sesquicentennial in 2008, and so in 2007 I was inspired to submit a nomination for the planned anniversary exhibit, named "MN 150," at the Minnesota History Center. The special exhibit was to include the 150 people and factors that most influenced Minnesota.

My nomination, the Homesteader, was not a winner. Ironically, this nomination was among the winners: the Grasshopper! Surely, the selections were made by a group of "city slickers" who spent their lives in air-conditioned museums and never had to grow their own food or butcher their own meat. Food is supermarket produce. It is always reliably there when one is hungry, right?

Yes, my fellow Americans, the hard working Homesteader was not selected as a winning factor in Minnesota's history, but the destructive Grasshopper was. Perhaps it's because a grasshopper is green, and you can make a giant plastic one that children can sit on in a museum exhibit. What's exciting about immigrant homesteaders who work hard and keep to their own business? Now a grasshopper that flies in a giant swarming cloud of locusts that arrives unexpectedly and devours an entire crop along with the clothes off the clothesline; that's awesome!

Grasshoppers were considered a plague in the 1870s, when my immigrant great-great-grandparents Hochbaum and great-grandparents Gärtner arrived from South Russia. The years that grasshoppers attacked Minnesota farms included 1857, 1858, 1864, 1874, 1875, 1876, 1877, and then again in the early 1930s. I believe my Prussian great-grandparents Jahnke may have moved from Nicollet County to Cottonwood County by 1880 because of the grasshopper problem. Poison was used to battle the grasshoppers, and the disasters made victims of farmers who were unable to readily obtain assistance from families and communities due to the extensive damage caused by several consecutive years of disasters. State and federal resources were eventually allocated to assist the farmers that lost their crops. A day of prayer was also held in April 1877. I believe my great-great-grandparents Hochbaum settled on a homestead that was forfeited by a previous homesteader, probably driven away by the grasshoppers.

As a tribute to my four generations of ancestors that lived off the land of southwestern Minnesota, and grew food to feed their fellow Americans, I hereby share my "losing" nomination of the Homesteader as a significant factor in Minnesota's history.

The Homesteader

Homesteaders converted the tall grass prairie to farmland by plowing the virgin soil. The United States government required that at least ten acres of a farmer's homestead claim be plowed each year. Less than one percent of Minnesota's tillable land is now unplowed prairie, so complete was the land use change enacted by the homesteaders.

To give the homesteader a name, here is information from a homestead patent claim at the National Archives. It's for a widowed immigrant woman, Regina "Jennie" Deutschmann, to highlight the contributions that were made by hard-working women who were never honored during their lifetime for being anything special. I found this claim while looking at the papers of her late husband's brothers who came to America from Russia in the late 1870s.

Jennie's Homestead

To prove up on the homestead claim filed by her late husband, Regina (Jennie) Zöller Deutschmann became a naturalized citizen by renouncing her allegiance to the Czar of Russia, Alexander II, as documented in the Federal Bureau of Land Management record collection, Government Land Office homestead application files.

Regina Zöller was born in Kirschwald, South Russia, in 1838, the daughter of German colonists in the Grunau Colony. She married Georg Deutschmann (born in 1833) about 1856, and they immigrated to America with their nine children in 1879, settling in southern Minnesota, where four of five of Georg's siblings who immigrated in 1875 had settled.

Georg Deutschmann died the day before his forty-eighth birthday, just twenty-four days after filing his intent to homestead in 1881. Cause of death was an accident involving a farm animal. His widow, Jennie, proved up on his homestead claim in 1888, with the help of her five children living with her then. When the homestead was proved, her unmarried children were

Paulina, aged eight; Jacob, aged twelve; Helena, aged fourteen; Gottfried, aged nineteen; and Peter, aged twenty-three. Jennie also had two sons and a daughter who were married in the mid-1880s, and probably lived with her during the early homestead years. The eldest son was married in Russia.

Jennie was widowed with an infant and seven older children five decades before Social Security was available to provide federal assistance, leaving her to be self-reliant on the homestead. When asked when she was absent from the homestead she replied, "Only to go to town on business or to church," as recorded on the claim submitted by the Land Office.

Neighbor Ben Tabert, age thirty-two, testified that he had known Jennie for twenty-five years in Russia, and since 1879 as his neighbor in Rosehill. Neighbors Philip Ewy and Ludwig Jahnke testified that they observed Jennie and her children working on the land. Ludwig Jahnke stated that he had helped her with harvest and threshing, and that he and his family had visited her family "all day" on their farm on June 10, 1888. This was, of course, a Sunday, their day of rest. Mrs. Deutschmann and her children probably relished this day of rest from their farming of eighty acres, which had produced nine years of crops when homestead proof was provided in 1888. Crops included wheat, oats, flax, barley, and potatoes. Ten acres were broken in 1879, thirty-five acres in 1880, and additional acreage broken each year after that.

Jennie died two months before her eightieth birthday, and was buried in the prairie cemetery at Rosehill Emmanuel Cemetery, Cottonwood County, Minnesota.

Jennie listed her farm equipment as: a breaking plow, stirring plow, seeder, harrow, mower, binder, and a hay rake used one to seven years. Her livestock included four horses, fifteen cattle, forty-five sheep, and four hogs.

While the Minnesota Historical Society never honored the Homesteader in their Sesquicentennial museum exhibit, I remember and honor Regina (Jennie) Deutschmann, the widowed prairie homesteader, with a flower for her gravestone on Memorial Day.

Rosehill Emmanuel Lutheran Cemetery, Rosehill Township, Cottonwood County, Minnesota. (Photo Courtesy of Nancy Gertner)

As I Remember It, 1912 – 1992

Jake Klotzbeacher

My father, Gottfried Klotzbücher, was born in Beresina, Bessarabia (in South Russia), in 1883. His grandfather, Ulrich Klotzbücher moved to Beresina from Gündelbach, Wurttemburg, Germany, at the invitation of Czar Alexander I, grandson of Catherine the Great. My father, Gottfried, served in the Russo-Japanese war of 1905-06.

In 1910 Gottfried Klotzbücher came to North Dakota with his cousins Jacob and Christina (Schramm) Schlauch. A matchmaker *(Kuppelsmann)* found my father a bride, Miss Louise Gulke. They made their home on her one-hundred-sixty acre homestead, near Forbes, Dickey County, North Dakota, already equipped with a claim shanty, some cattle, horses, hogs, chickens, geese, and some machinery. I was born on that homestead November 30, 1912.

During my growing up years, we moved back and forth from the homestead near Forbes to the little town of Merricourt, North Dakota. In sixteen years, seven more siblings were born to my parents.

We had all the normal childhood diseases such as chicken pox and measles. I can't give enough credit to our mother. She saw to it that we had our three meals a day. I'll never know how she did it. She always managed a small garden and a potato field, got us kids to do the hoeing, and there were always enough animals to butcher in the fall for meat. We preserved the meat in a large crock. We also made sausage which we smoked and hung in the attic where it kept all winter. We made something we call a *Pressmagen*. The animal's stomach was cleaned out and then stuffed with precooked ground meat and flavored with spices such as garlic, oregano *(Pfefferkraut),* salt, and pepper. Then it was put between a couple of boards and a heavy rock was placed on it for a couple of weeks. After that you could slice it off in slabs. It was delicious.

Mother was a great cook and baker, particularly with the primitive equipment she had to make things with. On top of all this, she was crippled. Her right leg was about four inches shorter than her left due to an accident which she and her brother, Jake, had when she was a girl of about eighteen or so. They upset a load of hay and Mother's hip was put out of joint. It could have been easily fixed, but in those days, no one was available with the medical wisdom to put it back in the socket. She spent the rest of her life in that condition.

Mother had many other talents such as sewing and crocheting which was fortunate for us kids. We seldom received any new clothes. Mother would cut up old clothes, use the good parts, and sew shirts, pants, dresses, etc. for us. She would knit stockings and mittens for us by unraveling old sweaters. Most of the footwear we had was ill-fitting hand-me-downs from people who had no more use for them.

We kids were warned about Gypsies roaming through the area. They were mostly horse traders coming down the road in covered wagons with strings of horses, kids, and dogs, pots and pans – everything they possessed. When they arrived we tried to lock up everything. Gypsies were shrewd and always came out ahead when trading horses. They cooked by campfire wherever they stopped and were great musicians, using accordions, fiddles and guitars.

I graduated from the eighth grade in 1927. Sometimes I wonder how I ever made it. I was kept from school for work much of the time, had no books to study from, no library to consult, no magazines, no newspapers or radio, and lived out in the boondocks. It helped that I lived from 1919 to 1923 in Merricourt and learned to speak English well because other students were English speakers.

In those days roads weren't much more than Indian trails. There were few cars. If you wanted to go someplace, you took the shortest route across fields and pastures. There were pasture gates at every place which you opened and closed as you went. We had no gravel or paved roads in our part of Dickey County.

Very few groceries were bought in town, just the bare necessities like salt, sugar, and items we couldn't make or grow ourselves. At home wild and locally raised berries were made into jams, jellies, and sauces. Meats were preserved by being fried down and stored in large stone crocks. Vegetables were eaten fresh in season. The rest were canned. Carrots and beets were put in sand and kept in a storm cellar or basement along with the canned goods. The hams and sausage were smoked and hung in the attic where it was dry. Flour and sugar were bought in large quantities; one-hundred pounds of sugar was a normal purchase and perhaps one-thousand pounds of flour in one-hundred-pound bags. My folks used to trade wheat for flour at the flour mill in Kulm, North Dakota.

Buffalo were killed off in our area by 1900, but in the hilly country where I grew up, we had a lot of small ponds where ducks were plentiful. Prairie chickens, grouse, and geese came through the area in the fall on their way south. Pheasants were introduced in the 1930s. My brother, Klotzie, and I managed to hunt enough in season to keep plenty of wild game on the table.

New Year's was something everyone looked forward to. It was a break from the drudgery of everyday life. The Germans from Russia pioneers brought over a custom, a method of celebrating the New Year that commenced after midnight. All households prepared extra food and alcoholic beverages and after midnight would expect a rap on their bedroom window indicating that there were "New Year's Shooters" (*Neujahr Schießer*) outside ready to bring in the New Year. The *Neujahr Schießer* were young men in the neighborhood armed with shotguns who would arrive at each residence by sled or horseback reciting one or more of the following New Year's greetings.

Nun ist das Neue Jahr gekommen,
Hab' ich es mir vorgenommen,
Euch zu wünschen in der Zeit
Friede, Glück and Einigkeit.

59

(Now that New Year has arrived, I am determined to wish you peace, good fortune, and unity.)

Wenn ich Euch nur wünschen könnte
Was ich in meinem Herzen finde,
So viel Glück und so viel Segen
Fällt dann nur auf einen wegen.
Kehret dann in alle Häuser ein,
Leib und Seel' soll gesegnet sein.

(If I could only wish you what is in my heart, then may good fortune and blessings on your behalf enter every home and may body and soul be blessed.)

Ich wünche Euch ein Glückseliges Neues Jahr,
und ein langes Leben,
darauf solls Rauch and Feuer geben.

(I wish you a year filled with blessings, good fortune, and a long life sealed by fire and smoke.)

...and then they would shoot!

After all the wishing and shooting, the *Neujahr Schießer* were invited in and served all the goodies prepared for the occasion. After eating and drinking the best wine and schnapps, they would depart for the next farm. By dawn, most were so intoxicated that they would start falling out of their sleds.

There was normally a barn dance somewhere in the neighborhood on Saturday nights. People would come in every mode of transportation: horse and buggy, horseback, sled, Model T Fords as well as Dodges, Buicks, Reos, Whippets, and Chevrolets. The music consisted of fiddles, accordions, and banjos. We danced waltzes, fox trots, square dances, two-steps, and polkas. During Prohibition, drinking at these dances consisted of homemade moonshine. Occasionally someone got a hold of some Canadian whiskey that made its way across the Canadian border to our community.

From 1934 to 1936 the grasshopper infestation was almost beyond description. They were so numerous that they ate anything that stood above ground. They even chewed on fence posts until they looked as if someone deliberately painted them white. Wherever there was a stretch of paved road, it became slippery from cars running over the hoppers. When the hoppers moved from area to area, the shadow of their wings gave the appearance of a plastic curtain between the sun and the earth. You had to live through this to believe it!

I was living with my uncle John Gulke, who served on the local school board. Ethel Skoglund, from Guelph, North Dakota, was hired to teach. My cousin Wilbert, a student of Miss Skoglund, hounded her about meeting his cousin Jake Klotzbeacher. Miss Skoglund paid board and room at the neighbor Christ Miller's, but Uncle John invited her to spend the weekend at the family farm. After that, Uncle John let me use his car to take Ethel to movies and parties. On April 1, 1937, we became engaged. Sometimes I wondered about my state of mind. I had no money. In fact, I had to skin my Uncle John's dead cows to get money to purchase an engagement ring.

In the winter of 1936-37, we had at least three feet of snow on the level. People didn't have the means of opening the roads; snow removal equipment amounted to a horse-drawn road grader. Most townships only had one. As a result, people rarely got to town to pick up necessities like coal, sugar, salt, coffee, and kerosene. I was staying at my uncle John's and we were badly in need of supplies. Uncle John and our neighbor Christ decided to make a trip to town by sled.

It was a cold, sunny day, and it was eight miles into town. By the time they left town with a half-ton of coal and other supplies, it was three thirty p.m. and already getting dusk on that county trail. About a mile from home, the sleigh tipped over when a sudden blizzard struck without warning. They couldn't see anything ahead of them.

Uncle John had a flashlight which he used to check the weeds sticking through the snow so they knew where the road was. They unhooked the sleigh and Christ led the horses behind Uncle John. In this manner they plodded along until they got as far as Christ's mailbox, about fifty yards from the house. There they got a heck of a surprise.

When they weren't home by dark, my aunt and I didn't worry too much. We were certain that they stayed in town. Meanwhile I did all of my uncle's chores.

About eight thirty p.m., Uncle John appeared in the dark. He followed the fence line home from Christ's place and he proceeded to relate the other part of this story.

School had been held on this sunny cold day. At four p.m., John Pahl came by sleigh to pick up his children and he asked Ethel if she wanted a ride to Christ Miller's farm. She declined as it was nice out and it was the custom for the teacher to do her own janitor work, like banking the fire with coal to keep a little heat in the school room, sweeping up, cleaning the blackboard and erasers, correcting papers, etc.

About four thirty p.m., Ethel started home – a distance of half a mile. She hardly got under way when the blinding blizzard blew in. By the time she got as far as Christ's mailbox, it was so bad she couldn't see twenty feet ahead of her. "It was like sitting in a bottle of milk," she said. Ethel was afraid to leave the mailbox in fear of getting disoriented. She felt as long as she stayed by the mailbox, she knew where she was and someone would find her. It was three hours before Uncle John "bumped" into her. By this time Ethel was pretty well frostbitten. Fortunately, the temperature was about twenty degrees above zero so she wasn't frozen stiff! It was Ethel's good fortune that Uncle John and Christ didn't stay in town that day.

Excerpted, with permission, from Jake Klotzbeacher's memoir, "*As I Remember It, 1912 – 1992.*"

Jake Klotzbeacher, Farmington, Minnesota, Chief of Police.
(Photo courtesy of Donovan Klotzbeacher)

From Russia, *mit Liebe*

Bernelda Kallenberger Becker

"'From Russia, *mit Liebe*.' As members of the American Historical Society of Germans from Russia come to the Twin Cities this week for their annual convention..." This headline in the June 11, 1996, *Minneapolis StarTribune* Variety section caught my attention. The map featured in the article showed the areas in Russia where German immigrants had settled in the 1800s. A faint memory took me to my bookshelves where I located my hometown's 1937 *EUREKA 1887 – 1937* book. I turned to the short story about my grandfather on page 103. Yes! He *had* come to the United States and to Dakota Territory from Odessa, South Russia in 1885.

I made an impulsive decision. I cancelled my plans for the day and made my way to the Radisson South in Bloomington to see what this AHSGR was all about. I didn't expect the impact that chance sighting of a headline would have on my life. I learned AHSGR has their headquarters in Lincoln, Nebraska. They had trucked their library to the convention. It contained obituary cards, family history books, and marriage, birth, and death records. I felt like a child in a candy store with innumerable coins to spend.

I began with obituaries. I knew the least about my mother's family, and began my search with her father's name. His obituary led to my grandmother's. Both were in German. I had lost my German years before, even though I had spoken it as a child. I made copies, hoping to find someone who could translate them for me later. Before the week ended I was a member of the local North Star Chapter as well as AHSGR.

In a few short years I learned the fascinating history behind the immigration of thousands of these people to South Russia from Germany, and one hundred years later their immigration to the plains states of the United States and Canada. New friends and activities enriched my life. Long-lost relatives surfaced, each with their own fascinating stories to add to my expanding file.

I also became a member of a second organization, the Germans from Russia Heritage Society, headquartered in Bismarck, North Dakota. It was at one of their conventions I discovered one of my most valued gems of information—an oral interview of my grandfather's youngest sister, Sophia Beck. Funded by the Works Projects Administration (WPA) in Washington, D.C., field workers interviewed "old timers" to preserve their stories in 1939 and 1940. The original documents are available for use at the Historical Society of North Dakota in Bismarck. Her story provided details I had never known about. She told of their life in their South Russian village of Neuburg, their trip across the ocean, life in a sod house on the prairie, and the hardships they endured. I wept as I read.

Several years ago I spent several days in Eureka, South Dakota. I copied a wealth of information at the Eureka Pioneer Museum. I walked the cemetery filming tombstones—my great-grandparents, my grandparents, uncles, aunts, and cousins. I lunched in the Luncheonette, a restaurant that had survived the years. I took pictures—the building that had at one time housed the Eureka Bazaar, the hospital up on the hill where my Mama had been taken after my baby brother, Jimmy, was born at home, the church I attended as a child, the house Grandpa had lived in after he moved off the farm. I went to the homestead farm. The buildings are gone, but the few trees that were behind the barn still shade my stillborn little brother's grave.

A trip to Eureka's hometown newspaper, the *Northwest Blade*, led me to my father's auction sale notice in a yellowed, crumbling newspaper dated September 3, 1937. More tears as emotions I hadn't expected swept over me. I sold an article entitled "Dad's Auction" to *Good Old Days Specials*. Family and friends in various parts of the United States contacted me following its appearance.

Best of all, I have come to appreciate my ethnic heritage, one I had spurned since World War II when it was unpopular to be German. In 1934, when I began first grade, I spoke only German. By 1945, my sophomore year in high school, my main goal in life was to rid myself of my German accent.

I'm looking forward to the day I walk through those pearly gates of heaven. I hope to spend eternity with family I have never known. I hope and pray heaven has a universal language. I have pages and pages of questions, still unanswered, that only they can answer, and I still can't remember my German.

Previously published in the January 2004 Minnesota North Star Chapter Newsletter.

CHAPTER FOUR

Family

Salomea Job Dockter, born in Neudorf, South Russia,
with grandchildren and great-grandchildren,
rural Emmons County, North Dakota, circa 1920s.
(Photo courtesy of Carol Just)

Tradition

Shirley Keller Halvorsen

Something old – a wedding veil
something new – a dress
something borrowed – a string of pearls
and so the stage was set.

German heritage
dictated the format of the wedding.
A simple church ceremony
followed by a dinner and reception
prepared and attended by
the guests.

The menu was typical
for such a wedding feast
noodle soup and butterballs
roasted chicken
roasted beef and potatoes
rye bread
garlic sausage
fruit pies
and *kuchen*.

Many a toast was made
with schnapps and beer abound
the celebration had officially begun.

The band consisted of an accordion and dulcimer player
timeless polka melodies floated through the air as
the bride and groom began to dance.

They danced with pride and joy
this was <u>their</u> day
the guests joined in the dancing
being careful to pin money
on the bride in order
to dance with her.
As the evening progressed
her money purse had doubled in size
her guests were generous.

At midnight
a cold supper was served
with the same enthusiasm and appetite as the dinner.

The celebration was nearing the end.
The marriage contract had been sealed with
vows and
food and song and dance
and love.

Previously published in the North Star Chapter of Minnesota Newsletter,
Volume 9, Number 4, October 1985.

Grandmother's Lasting Influence

Bernelda Kallenberger Becker

Fredericka was her name, but to me she was "*Grossmutter*." My papa's mother lived about two city blocks from us, but not in a city. "*Grossvater*" had given his farm to my papa, and built a new farm on part of the land.

When Mama had to work in the fields, she put a few diapers in a bag and sent me over to *Grossmutter*. The only memory I can conjure up of that time is of the turkey gobbler who ruled her farmyard. He seemed as big or bigger than I was, and he strutted around with all his tail feathers on display. His wattle shook menacingly when he gobbled. He made a fearsome display, but I can't recall that he ever attacked me.

Things were more interesting at *Grossmutter's* house than at ours. For one thing, she had a Victrola. It had a prominent place in her parlor. She didn't have many records, but I particularly remember one she played many times. She would crank the Victrola and let me listen. I still recall some of the words of one song: "Tell Mother I'll be there, in answer to her prayer. Angels, tell my mother I'll be there."

The only book at our house was a Bible. Papa took the Aberdeen South Dakota, newspaper, and the mailman also delivered *The Dakota Farmer,* a farm magazine. Grandmother didn't have many books either, but she had one that left a deep impression on my child mind.

To look at it I had to sit on the stiff leather couch in the parlor. I was firmly admonished to turn the pages carefully so as not to tear them. Brightly colored pictures of heaven and angels filled some of the pages. But there were also scenes of the devil and his demons torturing humans who had been unfortunate enough to land in hell. Paging through the treasured book put the fear of God into me for many years to come.

The cellar at our house was dark, damp, and full of spiders. Grandmother's cellar wasn't much different except that she kept a cricket in her cellar for good luck. But if one managed to find its way into ours, Mama couldn't rest until she had put it out of its misery. *Grossmutter* had a room adjoining her cellar that was used as a kitchen in the summertime. She cooked and canned her vegetables there because it was cooler than her upstairs kitchen.

When she took fresh bread from the oven and put it on a rack, I'd beg for my favorite treat. After it cooled, she would cut a slice and take it to the cellar where she kept food that needed to be kept cool and put sour cream on it. Then she sprinkled it with sugar. I can still taste it. Mmm—good!

A wondrous attraction in her upstairs bedroom was a white horse-hair rug on the floor in front of the bed. If I removed my shoes she allowed me to play on it. I loved to stroke the soft hair and smell the tanned leather.

Most wondrous of all, *Grossmutter* had a bathroom! It didn't have a toilet (we still had to use the outhouse), but no one else I knew had a room set aside for bathing. Its furnishings included a vanity table with a three-sectioned mirror she could move so she could look at the sides of her hair as well as the front. On the vanity she kept a tortoiseshell comb and brush and a dish with a tortoiseshell cover into which she put the hair she removed from the brush. It was fascinating to watch *Grossmutter* brush her hair. When she removed the hairpins from her bun, her hair dropped to the middle of her back. Mama's hair was short and permed. I thought Grandmother's hair was prettier.

A bathtub took up most of the space in the bathroom. It was the only bathtub I had ever seen. There was no greater treat than a bath while I was at her house. Since the house had no running water, she would bring a bucket of warm water she had heated on the kitchen range. When I finished bathing, I pulled the plug, and the water ran outside.

Grossmutter had a little satchel ready by the door in the event some-one needed her services. Our community depended on her for simple medi-cal help when they had ailments or accidents. Of particular interest to me was a shiny cylinder, about the size of a flashlight. When you rubbed it on your body, the prickly sensation was frightening as well as pleasant. She said it was used for people whose muscles ached. I stood in awe of her skills and did not hesitate to bring my bumps and bruises to her.

God and church were important to *Grossmutter*. On Sundays I'd sit between her and Mama in church. The ladies sat on one side of the church and the men on the other. Grandmother would reach into her pocket and hand me a peppermint candy, usually covered with lint. I'd brush it off and enjoy the tasty treat. She would also allow me to page through her German hymnal. In it I'd find pressed flowers. A cellophane band with the word "Mother" printed on it in pink intrigued me. I handled it gently, admiring its beauty. The only memento I have of my grandmother is that hymnal, still containing that cellophane band.

Grossmutter died in 1938 when I was nine years old. Her death left a big void in my young life. But her influence bore fruit throughout my teenage years, because when temptations assailed, I would think of her prayers.

Fredericka Hof Kallenberger
(Photo courtesy of Bernelda Kallendberger Becker)

Now I've lived more years than she did. I realize she was just as human, just as likely to make mistakes, just as imperfect as I am now. But I'll never cease to be thankful for the part she played in forming my values.

Previously published in *Good Old Days Specials*, March 2000.

Otto H. Froh,
Founder and Publisher of the *Eureka Rundschau*
Joan Froh

Although my paternal grandfather, Otto H. Froh, was not German Russian, he had quite a profound influence on the ability of this ethnic group to gather information about their forbears. He and Gustav Mauser established a German weekly, the *Eureka Rundschau,* in 1912 in Eureka, South Dakota. This newspaper served as a link for communication between the German Russian immigrants in the United States and their relatives who still lived in the German colonies of South Russia. As such, it now serves as a valuable source of historical and genealogical information for us descendants of the Germans from Russia and is an excellent aid in documenting our heritage.

Otto H. Froh was born in Hamburg, Germany, on December 3, 1878. He was one of thirteen children, but only six survived to school age. At age fifteen, shortly after the death of his mother, he began serving a four-year apprenticeship as a printer. This culminated in a craftsman degree in that trade.

When Otto's father, my great-grandfather, immigrated to the United States in 1895, he left the youngest of his children in foster care. Otto had no desire to follow. However later, when his father offered him free transportation to join him, Otto's spirit of adventure prompted him to set sail for America. My father, Walter Froh, in an article about his father, Otto Froh, published on June 21, 1962, for the seventy-fifth anniversary of the *Eureka Northwest Blade* wrote*:* "Arriving in New York he boarded a westbound train. As he passed through town after town he was impressed and intrigued by the numerous store fronts displaying the sign 'General Merchandise.' Not very well versed in the English language, he came to the conclusion that this General by the name of Merchandise must indeed be a very wealthy man to own so many stores."

He arrived in March 1901 and joined his father, Johann, at his farm homestead near Rolla, North Dakota. He remained there for eight months and helped put in one crop, but he became restless and chose to leave to follow his printing trade. After visiting relatives in St. Paul, Minnesota, he went south on a train and found employment in Mountain Lake, Minnesota, where he began work as a German-language compositor on a weekly newspaper.

While in Mountain Lake he met and married my grandmother, Barbara Koehn, the daughter of German Prussian Mennonites who emigrated from the Molotschna colonies of South Russia. Her ancestors had settled in Russia in the early 1800s following an invitation from Catherine the Great and later, Czar Alexander I. This area is north of the Sea of Azov in what is present-day Ukraine.

In order to better himself financially, in 1910 Otto moved his family to Eureka, South Dakota, where he became a co-editor of a German weekly, *The Volkszeitung*. In 1912 he severed connections with that publication, and he and Mr. Mauser established the *Eureka Rundschau*. The new German weekly grew and prospered with a subscription list of nearly five thousand. It circulated as freely among the Germans in South Russia as it did with their relatives all over the United States. Many of the published letters from Russia in the 1920s were heart-wrenching, telling of famine, starvation, and extreme deprivation. They often begged American relatives for food, money or clothing. Following is just one such letter from Michael and Christina Bindewald, Neu-Beresina, South Russia, published in the *Rundschau* dated June 22, 1922:

> *"First the crop failure and second, we had everything taken away. We have no more livestock to sell, having only two cows remaining. If there is no help from another country, then we are lost. Throughout the whole winter, we have had only two meals each day, and a man cannot endure this for a long time. There are eight in our family; we have sent to Poland all the clothes we could sell for food. Pleading for your assistance."*

Home of Northwest Blade
and Eureka Rundschau

**Northwest Blade and Eureka Rundschau building.
(With permission from the Germans
from Russia Heritage Collection, NDSU Libraries,
Fargo – www.ndsu.edu/grhc)**

When World War I broke out in 1914, and with Russia as an eventual combatant, a decline in circulation began as foreign mail service deteriorated. During this period and following the Russian revolution in 1917, contacts with the German people in South Russia became difficult. Eventually the correspondence between these colonies and their relatives in America was completely cut off by the Bolsheviks. Because of this, the *Rundschau* lost much of its appeal and circulation dwindled to less than two thousand. In addition, all national advertising in German publications ceased. This cut off the most important source of revenue.

Otto H. Froh, age forty-two
(Photo courtesy of Joan Froh)

During World War I, although my grandfather had become a naturalized citizen and was a patriotic American, the fact that he was German-born caused him to be under surveillance by the FBI. As a consequence, they also constantly scrutinized the German *Rundschau* for subversive matter. In addition, the FBI required a translation of front-page stories, comments, and editorials that had to be filed with the postmaster when they mailed each weekly issue. This became such a tedious task that such items were, of necessity, kept to a minimum which diminished the prestige of the paper and the interest of its subscribers.

After suffering continuous losses with the *Rundschau*, it was sold in 1926 to Leicht Publications of Winona, Minnesota. There it was combined with other German-language newspapers.

In 1917 Mauser and Froh had purchased the *Eureka Northwest Blade,* an English-language weekly. They published it for several years concurrently with the *Rundschau* until the latter was sold. After the sale, Otto took over sole ownership of the *Blade.* Although his formal education had been entirely in German, he had become proficient enough in the English language to edit an English newspaper. The paper flourished as did the city of Eureka, and my grandfather promoted and crusaded for the best interests of the city. However, with the onset of bank failures, the Great Depression, drought and crop failures, it became difficult to continue on. Under these extremely adverse conditions, Otto sold the *Northwest Blade* in 1936 and left Eureka, never to return. He and his family initially located to Chicago, but later settled in Michigan.

In August 1941 our family of four drove to Chicago to visit my grandfather Froh and other relatives. To defray the cost, we used one hundred silver dollars that my parents had saved. Since we had never before been to such a big city, and hadn't seen these relatives for four years, the trip was planned with great anticipation. Grandpa took us sightseeing and we were so amused because nearly everything we saw he described as being "the biggest in the world!" He took us to the airport where we were amazed while watching the huge planes take off and land. The push-button elevators in tall buildings were another fascination. This two-week trip was the only extended vacation our family ever took and it created wonderful memories, especially for me since it was the last time I ever saw my grandfather.

Otto H. Froh died on March 31, 1958, at the age of seventy-nine. Early in his lifetime he had endured the untimely death of his first wife, my grandmother. She died following childbirth in 1912 at the age of thirty-six. Grandfather was left with five young children, ages eight, four, three, one, and a newborn. He then married Katherina Weller in Eureka and together they had three more children.

When my father told us stories of his childhood, he reminisced of the fun he and his siblings had playing games with their father on Sunday afternoons. He would sing little German ditties and tell them about his own childhood when he lived in Hamburg, Germany. They sometimes would drive to the countryside in their touring car and picnic.

When Otto H. Froh sold the *Blade,* and left Eureka he did not dispose of the remaining copies of the *Rundschau*, published from 1912 to 1926. Instead, he stored them in the basement of the *Northwest Blade* building where they remained in good condition until retrieved by a later editor. They were subsequently donated to the Germans from Russia Heritage Society (GRHS) in Bismarck, North Dakota. There they were transferred to microfilm and became available for genealogical or other purposes. The North Dakota State Historical Society in Bismarck also has the microfilm available for research. This source has been noted at sessions of the American Historical Society of Germans from Russia (AHSGR), including the national convention in Minneapolis in 1996.

I doubt that Otto H. Froh ever imagined that the German newspaper he established in 1912 would become so meaningful and so appreciated by future generations of Germans from Russia in America.

My Mother's Kitchen Surprise

Merv Rennich

The aroma wafted up from the kitchen to my attic room where I was reading a Captain Marvel comic book. SHAZAM! Billy Batson had just become Captain Marvel, ready to take on the thugs of the lower East End who had been causing havoc that the local authorities could not control. The aroma was getting to me. I turned the page and could not stand it any longer. I had to see where the delicious smell was coming from. Captain Marvel had to wait as I rushed down the steep stairs and into the kitchen.

On the stove I saw a huge black and white-speckled kettle with a lid that was intermittently rattling as the steam escaped from its edge. I could not imagine what smelled so good! I said to myself, "I've got to see what it is!"

Being only seven years old, I slid a chair from the nearby kitchen table over to the stove and stood on it. Grabbing a potholder I lifted the rattling cover from the pot. When the steam cleared, I was more than just startled to see a pig's head staring at me with its snout, eyes, and ears just above the boiling liquid with garlic, cloves, onions, and bay leaves floating on the surface.

How disgusting! All of a sudden the aroma didn't smell so delicious anymore! I felt like throwing up!

I put the lid back, scrambled off the chair, and went down to the basement where I had been told an hour before to go to my room because I was in the way. Here my parents and my grandparents were finishing the butchering of a pig and a steer. One of the last processes was underway. It was grinding the meat (sausage) and getting it ready to stuff into the pig's small intestines that my mother had cleaned earlier. But before the stuffing could begin, the sausage had to be seasoned with salt, pepper, onion, and garlic, and probably some other spices.

My grandfather would strip down to the waist, thoroughly wash himself with soap and water, thrust his hands into the big tub of ground meat, and start mixing the reddish white mixture. It was sticky and would cling to his forearms up to his elbows. Every so often my grandmother would add some salt, pepper, onion, garlic, and whatever. Grandfather would mix some more until everyone agreed it was time to stop and see if the sausage was ready.

The only way to properly tell was to fry some and taste it. My mother made a rather large patty with her hands and then went up to the kitchen to fry it on the stove beside the big boiling pot. When finished she called down and everyone come up to have a taste and give their opinion as to whether it was just right or needed a little of this or a little of that. The taste of the sausage took away my thought of the pig's head boiling in the pot.

After cooking for a few hours, the pig's head was allowed to cool. Then the fleshy parts of the head were cut off, diced, and, with some other ingredients, stuffed into the pig's stomach and tied off. This my parents referred to as *Schwatamaga* or head cheese. It was a German family custom brought over from the "old country," Russia. My father was born in Waterloo in the Beresan District northeast of Odessa, and my mother's family immigrated from Hoffnungstal, Bessarabia.

For the following several days I had to keep the fire in the smoke house going so it could do its job curing the sausages and the *Schwatamaga* which, of course, I never did eat because every time it was mentioned or I looked at it, all I could see was a pig's head in a pot staring at me.

Be Loyal, Buy Smucker's Jams

John Hafner

I cannot truthfully tell you that I grew up in a Germans from Russia community, but I can tell you about growing up in Lutheran communities, with Lutheran pastors as parents and grandparents who fit that category. I can tell you that our North Star Chapter of Minnesota meets in the Berea Lutheran Church of Richfield, Minnesota, a church that in the mid-forties began its life as a mission church with my father, Herbert Hafner, as the pastor. When the congregation first assembled and needed a name for their new church, it was my mother's suggestion to name it Berea Lutheran. The word Berea comes from Paul's writings in the Book of Acts.

I began life as a Canadian in 1942. My father was a Lutheran pastor in Alberta. When I was the tender age of about six weeks my parents accepted a call to pastor at Christ Lutheran Church in Eagan, Minnesota, at that time called Nichols.

My mother, Margaret Fiess Hafner, had many interesting stories to tell about her father, Traugott Fiess, and the life they lived in the various Lutheran parishes as she grew up. My grandfather Fiess had a strange name—Traugott means "Trust in God." He was born in May 1883 in Sarata, in the Russian province of Bessarabia. Research tells us Sarata, a mostly Lutheran community, was founded in 1822 by immigrants from Württemberg and Bavaria, Germany. As a young man he made plans to immigrate to America where several relatives were already established. I have a copy of his most fascinating autobiography filled with firsthand anecdotes in which he tells of life in Bessarabia, passage on the ship, and his first several months in the Utica, Michigan, area where his uncle Schoech had settled. His uncle was a Lutheran pastor and suggested Traugott attend a Lutheran seminary in Springfield, Illinois, as there was an acute shortage of pastors. He and a cousin, John Schmucker Jr., arrived at Springfield to begin classes at the seminary in September 1903.

Check out the preserves shelves in your favorite grocery—notice the "Smucker" labels? Yes. These Smuckers are the very same Schmucker family. My mother quipped that they changed their name to be shorter so it would fit the label on the jar. In a letter from 1877, when apparently business wasn't booming, Grandfather Schmucker wrote "People have no money. They are buying very little. Plow handles have a pretty good price at five cents apiece." He asked his son-in-law to find a sub-agent for his smoking pipes. Spinning wheels sold for one dollar each.

Several years and many interesting events later, Traugott Fiess's seminary time ended and the time came for assignment to a parish. Traugott was assigned to Gresham, Shawano County, Wisconsin. Here my grandmother, Anna Gesine Harms, enters the picture. Traugott was to come to his new parish with a wife! He and Anna had sort of an agreement, but while in Seminary, student engagements were not permitted. Anna's parents thought she was too young to be a pastor's wife, but love won out and they were married on August 22, 1909. Thus began my grandfather Traugott's lifetime career as a pastor in Lutheran parishes in Wisconsin.

My mother was Traugott and Anna's first child, born June 8, 1910, at the parsonage. They named her Margaret (Pearl) Johanna (God's gift). How I wish there were room in this short essay to relate the many interesting anecdotes my grandfather recorded in his autobiography, and told by aunts and uncles. I do have to include just one story that my aunt Vicki included in an oral interview conducted by the Minnesota Historical Society. Her mother, Anna Fiess, my grandmother, sewed most of her children's clothes. Vicki had only two school dresses when she started first grade. Most houses had no closets, so the few clothes they had hung on a hook, probably behind the door.

She told how during the days of the Great Depression, there were no extra dollars or even pennies for "luxuries" such as running water or electricity. Besides being a great pastor, Grandfather Fiess was innovative and ever

**Traugott and Anna (Harms) Fiess on their wedding day,
August 22, 1909.**
(Photo courtesy of Joanne Stark)

mindful to make unique solutions to everyday living challenges. He put a stock watering tank upstairs above the kitchen. It was somehow connected to a tank that held the water, and there were pipes coming from that tank to the firebox in the wood stove in the kitchen. In the wintertime when there was fire in the stove there was hot water too. He figured out a way to have some electricity also. He put a wind charger on top of the garage. He had batteries in the garage that were charged by the wind. A wire ran over to the house which carried enough electricity to light a bulb hanging in the kitchen, and Vicki said, she thinks one in the pantry and one in the bathroom.

My aunt Vicki Butler, in that same oral interview, mentioned the little village they called Budsin, north of Neshoro, Wisconsin. It had a church, a school, the town hall, a feed mill, and an old-fashioned general store with one gas pump. There were only four houses.

I remember seeing that general store when we visited there many years later. By then it was just an intersection with the old general store, now sort of a museum. I was intrigued with the barrels that had held food such as rice, beans, etc. The proprietor would measure it out and bag it for customers to take home, the sort of thing I saw on old Westerns on TV. The gas pump Aunt Vicki mentioned was one of the old type I have since seen when I've traveled the rural roads of our country. I think that somehow the gas would be pumped up into this glass container on top of the pump. Evidently gravity then allowed it to flow through the hose to fill the gas tank.

I had a great three months staying with my Fiess grandparents in Budsin. It was the time of the polio epidemic in the Twin Cities. My parents sent me there for safekeeping. Thankfully it was a wise move, and I did not get polio, plus I had the wonderful opportunity to hear some of Grandpa's reminiscences and got to know him better. While I stayed with them, Grandpa took me fishing on Green Lake. First, we gathered bait by netting minnows along the sand beach. We were in a rowboat, and Grandpa let me have a turn at rowing, but I went in circles because I didn't refer to a landmark. We put the fish we caught in an old onion bag and hung it over the side of the boat. This worked for a while until a turtle ate a hole through the bag and all our fish got out. Another time I wanted to trap some rabbits. Grandpa Fiess built a box trap out of pallet lumber and chicken wire with trapdoors that slid down. When the rabbit pushed on the bait, a cob of corn, the string was released and the doors fell.

Grandfather Fiess was also artistic, and made beautiful cathedral-type lamps using stained glass. My parents, at the time, were involved in Berea Lutheran Church in Minneapolis, and my mother asked him if he could make some for Berea. They were removed when Berea was replaced with a new structure. My sister and I were fortunate to each acquire one of them.

Back to my father, Pastor Herbert Hafner. While traveling he spent some time in Milwaukee, Wisconsin, where he became acquainted with Renata Meyer, who introduced him to her roommate. The two young ladies were teaching there at the time. That young lady happened to be my mother, Margaret Fiess. They struck up a romance, but alas, Herb had to return to Alberta, Canada, where he was a Lutheran Missionary in Sexsmith, Grand Prairie, Alberta. Three years of love letters ensued until they were finally married with, as she said, having seen her "husband-to-be" in person a combined total of only eleven days. Our family has those love letters. They are deeply treasured. She told us children they often traveled to his Alberta churches via horseback because the roads were impassible by car. An opportunity opened for my father to pastor Christ Lutheran in Eagan, Minnesota, which brings me back to where I began—baby John Hafner coming to Minnesota in my mother's arms at the tender age of six weeks old.

The Genealogist's Table

Sharon Chmielarz

A tiny stage barely lit.
Dates, charts, bulky
as furniture
being shoved around.
Yellowed letters, snapshots
numbered
like beloved sand.
you like to know Wear We are Boarn?

And memory: a woman
firing a clay oven, feeding it
twisted slough hay,

children leading
a horse around a pole,
a dingy carrousel,
shaping the barn's dung
and straw into bricks for burning,

a man, following a trail
the Lakota made across the river.
The ice, like rubber.

Outside the window

the night hawk calls

from the creeks

Worthless and Rabbit.

amarca this countrey uncle Sam

(Photo courtesy of Carol Just)

From the Volga to the Mississippi

Sharon Chmielarz

(adaptation of "Volga German-Russians in Minnesota,"

Carol Just. *AHSGR Journal.* Summer. 1991.)

L et's say you were a German farmer in 1763 and heard that Catherine the
Great, a German princess, had become Czarina of all the Russias. You
heard she was offering special privileges to German farmers if they'd immigrate to Russia. Do you listen to your roving heart or your head?

You could never pass the promise of a good deal up. Free land. Free
transportation. Freedom to practice any trade you wanted. Freedom from
taxes and custom duties.

You packed up and moved to the Volga River. All was not as rosy as
painted. No seed provided for crops. No cows or oxen but plenty of wolves
to guard against with firearms and night fires. Thieves, too. But you stayed,
living along the Volga for a hundred years because with determination and
work your farm and your neighbors' become prosperous and peaceful.

Peace never lasts; along comes new, harsh Russian regulations. And
just in the nick of time new lands opened in the United States under the
Homestead Act. Say you talked the future over with your neighbors and
family. Many threw up their hands in horror. They'd never been farther
than twenty miles from home. But you pulled up stakes and emigrated. You
weren't alone. Thousands arrived at settlements in Nebraska, Iowa, Chicago,
Wisconsin, Saskatchewan. You landed in Minnesota.

Conveniently there was work there to be had. The St. Paul stockyards. The sugar beet circuit. Factories and foundries. Railroads stretching
east and west over the prairie. German colonies in Russia like Reinwald and
Schäfer are replaced by Minnesota towns like Gaylord, Glencoe, Arlington,
Winthrop, Hutchinson, and Ward 6 in St. Paul called Riverview, magnets
attracting immigrants and becoming the new "home."

Oh, *ja*. *das unkrout hat keine chance mit der grossmutter in den rote rube feld* (weeds don't stand a chance with grandmother in the beet field.)

In 1912 Jacob Ertel and his bride Emalia (Mollie) Schmidt used money saved for the customary three-day wedding to pay for passage to America. Mollie grieved leaving her parents' home in Schäfer for her father, Heinrich Schmidt, had the status and comfortable brick house of a wealthy man in their colony. Before she leaves *Vater* gives her a feather from one of his peacocks. So she won't forget him.

What if you were Mollie? Your letters finally persuade your parents to emigrate and join you and Jacob. The Schmidts leave Russia in 1921 but get no farther than Saratov, a port on the Volga, where they die of diphtheria. You are broken-hearted. When you are an old woman you still have the feather in your Bible.

Or put yourself in John Mohrlandt's boots, born in Russia, emigrated as a toddler with his parents. But your mother sighs to return, to spend her days with loved ones. So be it, but after she dies in Russia you return to the U.S. You marry eventually, set up business as a painter, and have nine children with Emalia Krumm in St. Paul. You will never see your mother's grave or the German colony again. In fact, you will fight as an American against Germans in WWI.

All was not sadness. Where it existed, melancholy was interrupted by card playing, singing, dancing, three-day celebrations. At the Schaeffers' three-day wedding, a guest wore out her shoes dancing. And though Prohibition reigned in the U.S. from 1919 to 1933, the Germans, used to making beer, whiskey and schnapps from their grain and wine from their vineyards, had access to a bootlegger, Mert Gallagher, who used her charm and probably a few bucks under the table to keep police eyes away from her operation and customers.

Churches were busy, too. Clever Catherine the Great had stipulated that all the colonies in Russia be settled by people of one denomination. This cut down on intra-faith arguments. The Emmanuel Evangelical Lutheran

Church on Humboldt Avenue and Dearborn Street in St. Paul was established already in 1873. The Deutsche Volkskirche in St. Paul, on the corner of Clinton and Congress became in 1895 another home for immigrant Germans' social and spiritual life.

And now, let's say you are a descendent of any of the Volga German immigrants. And really you're just getting adjusted to the fact that a vast history stands behind you. It could be coincidence or fate that you were born here. You intuit the past vaguely from some foods that came out of your great-great grandmother's kitchen: *einlauf soup, borscht, vareniki, kraut bierochs, runzas, kuchen, grebbel.* And you want to learn more, if only to sample these foods and to sing some of the old German hymns. It's your legacy, and it's calling to you.

SS Aller (1885)
(Steamship Historical Society Collection,
University of Baltimore Library)

CHAPTER FIVE

Townies

Parade in Wishek, North Dakota, circa 1920s.

(Photo courtesy of Frieda Just)

May Day 1945

Patsy Ramberg

Warm sun, melty, sloppy streets,
    VE Day is on the way,
Baskets of candy and cookies
To drop at best friends' doors.

VE Day is on the way,
Bird-like paper napkin baskets
To drop at best friends' doors,
Get caught and you get kissed.

Bird-like paper napkin baskets
Fall beside gold-starred doors,
Soldier, brother, father lost,
VE Day is on the way.

Fallen beside gold-starred doors,
Candy, cookies for broken families,
Soldier, brother, father forever beyond the sea,
Warm sun, melty, sloppy streets.

Author's note:

Giving May Baskets on May 1 was a custom now largely forgotten. In the 1940s, children left baskets filled with candy and other goodies on a friend's doorstep, then ran away quickly. The friend would run after the child, and if caught, give him/her a kiss.

Gold Star flags were hung in the windows of homes of families who had lost a son or father in WWII.

VE Day came on May 8, 1945. It means Victory over Europe, ending WWII.

John Graf Jr., my grandfather, lamented the war in a letter to his daughter, Katie, saying:

"This is a terrible war."

He was born in the village of Neudorf; his wife, my grandmother, Katerina Buck, was born in the village of Friedenstahl. They immigrated in the 1870s and farmed near Streeter, North Dakota. The poem is a pantoum, a form from Malaya which repeats lines in a certain order.

The Eureka Bazaar

Bernelda Kallenberger Becker

At age eight my Mall of America was the Eureka Bazaar. Oh, the wonders it held for this little farm girl on the Saturday night shopping trip to town. Ready-made dresses, patent leather shoes, store-bought bread. The promise of this weekly jaunt helped while away the long endless days on the farm.

Papa, dressed in nearly new striped bib overalls, and wearing his suit coat, would load the full can of cream and the crate of eggs on the back seat of his Model A Ford. I sat on the front seat between my parents, and amused myself during the four-mile drive watching the odometer count the miles. The four miles over gravel road at thirty miles per hour seemed endless.

Our first stop would be the creamery. The cream sold for cash. I waited with anticipation. Would Papa give me a nickel, or maybe even a dime when he returned to the car? Usually it turned out to be a nickel.

Mama traded the crate of eggs for groceries at the Bazaar. She would stand at the counter and tell the clerk what she wanted. He would record the item and its price on a slip of paper, and then place it in our empty egg crate. He measured food, such as dry beans sold in bulk, into paper bags. He then would add up the total. I never tired of watching the process of payment. If someone paid with cash, the clerk placed the money into a cylinder which he inserted into a vacuum tube. It whooshed upstairs to a tiny office where a cashier made change, if needed, and whooshed the cylinder back—truly a wonder to behold!

The important business of the evening taken care of, Mama was free to browse the store. I particularly remember how she and I would wander nonchalantly to a part of the store where on display was a beautiful blue porcelain coffeepot. It had an aluminum stem as its base, and the little percolator glass at the top had sort of a milk glass look. We looked at it every Saturday night, truly a luxury item that didn't belong in a farm house. But I could tell she really liked it. She would lift it up, pretend to pour a cup of coffee, and check out the percolator innards. Then she would put it down and we'd move on. I don't remember what it cost but it was too expensive, that's for sure.

Then, there came a Saturday night when something new had been added to that coffee pot—a little slip that stated "On Sale." I can just imagine how her heart must have leaped a bit to see that. She checked the new price, shook her head, and we continued on. This continued for several Saturday nights. She must have worried during the week. Did the desire for that beautiful item also lurk in the heart of one or two of the town ladies? Were they watching for more price reduction too? Would it be gone come the next Saturday night trip to town?

Then, one Saturday night, the price must have been just right, or maybe Mama had been squirreling away a bit of the egg money—we came home from Eureka with that coffee pot! I don't recall her making coffee in it—she must have. But one of the few heirlooms I have is that coffee pot. It's just as pretty as the day she purchased it, but I can't make coffee in it because I left it on the stove burner too long and ruined the inside.

Mama's blue coffee pot.
(Photo courtesy of Bernelda Kallenberger Becker)

Earlier in the evening I would meet my cousin Elaine, who had come to town with her parents. We usually had an agonizing decision to make at the candy counter. Whatever we spent our usual nickel or unusual dime on would have to last all evening, and hopefully, we'd have some sweets left over to take home.

While the mamas sat on a row of chairs and visited near their filled egg crates lined up by the door, Elaine and I sometimes made our way to the Millinery Department to try on hats if no one was there to stop us. The grown-up hats were beautiful, especially if they had a veil or feathers for decorations. We pretended we were movie stars and admired one another.

Our farmer papas spent their evening visiting the Pool Hall. Good Germans that they were, beer flowed freely while they shared farm news. By the time the men came to collect their wives, children, and the groceries, the drive home did not always go well. However, that never dampened my enthusiasm for the next shopping trip to town and the Eureka Bazaar.

Published in the North Star Chapter Newsletter April 2001, and the *Eureka Northwest Blade*, August 22, 2001.

Mercer's First Television Set

James Gessele

Conservative to the core, spare of words, and short in limb and stature, my father, Ted, could be a trailblazer nevertheless. A feat that gained him notoriety came in early 1952, when he became McLean County's first owner of a new gadget called television. This was before television transmission was even available in the state. It was also a moment when his German Russian upbringing whispered admonitions about arrogance and other words of caution lest he introduce some sinful element in the community. In the end, the Devil made him do it.

Already in 1951, the idea of "adding pictures to sound" fascinated residents of the state, at a time when the Federal Communications Commission anticipated granting hundreds of broadcasting licenses to qualified applicants. By then, Twin Cities, Minnesota, broadcasters were well on their way with this innovative means of communication. But North Dakota stations would have to wait their turn well into 1952 before their applications would even be considered. Under such a timetable, applicants realized that local television stations at best couldn't become fully operational until 1953, and station owners (usually owners of radio stations) set out to hype interest with air-time slogans. Who can forget radio station KFYR in Bismarck with its on-the-hour buzz of "TV in '53?"

A few people were so caught up in the fever they couldn't wait. In late 1951, some nut—I can't recall his name—in Bismarck's south-side warehouse district had a complete set-up aimed at capturing elusive Twin Cities' signals: a television receiver and an antenna that reached to the clouds, yet escaped nearby Bismarck Airport FAA height regulations. My father made the mistake of visiting this warehouse and immediately falling under the spell of the TV zealot—never mind that picture reception was nil. Each subsequent business trip to Bismarck was accompanied with a side visit to "The Nut."

In the meantime, the KFYR sloganeering had its intended effect, and in the winter of 1952 my father could no longer hold out.

Through Schell's Hardware he secretly ordered an Admiral console model television with radio and phonograph—in limed oak cabinetry in keeping with my mother's scheme of décor. Gleefully he anticipated delivery, until one morning at the usual nine a.m. men's coffee *klatsch* at Sam's Café, Julius Sackman, local Northern Pacific rail agent, stormed in and with loud disdain bellowed that "some damn fool has taken shipment of a TV, and a big one to boot." There was no room to hide behind a coffee cup; Dad had been "outed!"

His exposure at Sam's Café that morning paled next to what he had to bear once he began erecting a rooftop antenna. It began with an ordinary twenty-five-foot mast that quickly expanded to fifty feet once it was determined there was no hope for a signal with the puny version. With still no signal, the height was extended to a full seventy-five feet with a rotor apparatus, and there it had to stop—TV reception or not. The antenna was anchored to the Gessele residence rooftop with guy wires, and the roof was groaning during spells of stiff prairie winds.

The community looked on in amusement and amazement. Without even a hint of a picture signal as a sign of success, surely they felt my father had turned the corner as a rational being. But then they, too, got caught up in the magic, and soon school classmates made pilgrimages to our living room to gawk at a snowy screen just so they could attest they had seen Gessele's TV. "Fireside" gatherings of this nature around the glowing, snowy, blank tube continued, reaching a zenith when the Archie Kline family was invited in for after-Sunday-service lunch the fall of 1952. The meal was winding down, and the Kline's three-year-old Murray excused himself to "watch TV." Suddenly from the living room we heard the set blare forth with audio of a male voice. A stampede to the next room ensued, but all in vain. Somehow our set had captured a five-second snippet of a Minneapolis transmission that had strayed over Mercer territory, and we had all missed it—except Murray. The poor little fellow was hounded for an in-depth description of what he had witnessed. His truncated account of "a man with a black tie" left a lot to be desired. Even so, the event garnered a couple column-inches in the *Bismarck Tribune*.

Thanksgiving 1952, our family did get its first taste of television when we packed up and headed for Uncle Art's home in Minneapolis for the holiday. It was a novel time but such a huge let-down to return home, forced to wait almost another whole year before we had our own broadcasts. When they did arrive, it was a Minot station that beat KFYR to the punch. At first, low-wattage transmissions guaranteed extremely poor reception. But things improved over time, although viewing fare was limited an awful lot to old westerns and to kinescopes of East Coast live productions that we viewed a week later. That became old hat quickly, and soon KFYR was screaming another slogan: "Live in '55."

1955 photo of couple with new TV set.
(Photo courtesy of Carol Just)

The remaining course of early television broadcast is history, but my father was compelled to undertake one last fling. Not leaving well enough alone, he enrolled in a mail correspondence television repair course. Once enrolled, he learned to his consternation he needed knowledge of algebra, something his eighth-grade education had not provided. His country school education in a central North Dakota German Russian community had indeed been sorely lacking.

It wasn't without regret that he still harkened back to first grade and how he and his two classmates, Lydia Wall and cousin John Gessele, were still on page one of their primer in December 1921, all for lack of cooperating with the teacher (they spoke only German) and not speaking her language (English). He still chuckled when he recalled how the three conspired over Christmas holiday to tear out page one of the reader the minute school reconvened. It meant moving on and, if anything, gazing at the illustration on page two for the remainder of the year.

Nonplussed, Ted turned to Arlo Eckmann, a high school student at the time, to tutor him over the rough parts. He passed the course, and the countless hours he spent in repairing almost every set in the community are also history.

Previously published in the 2004 publication *Memories: Mercer, North Dakota,* a work commemorating the community's 2005 centennial anniversary.

"Just Chatting" in the *Ashley Tribune*

Joan Froh

My mother, Bertha Stock Froh, was a first-generation American, born of parents who immigrated to the United States from the German Glückstal colonies of South Russia. I'm not positive which of her ancestral generations first settled in Russia, but I believe it was her great-grandfather, Johannes Stock, in the early 1800s. Both his son and his grandson (my grandfather) bore the name Johann, a derivation of Johannes.

My grandfather, Johann Stock, born on January 27, 1863, in the village of Glückstal in South Russia arrived in the port of New York via Bremen, Germany, and Southampton, England, on board the SS EMS on April 22, 1889. The ship's manifest states that he was twenty-six years old and a "laborer." In the company of other Glückstal immigrants he traveled to Eureka, Dakota Territory, by train. They arrived there on April 27, 1889. His entire wealth consisted of twenty-five cents and a prized tobacco box. Johann, who later anglicized his name to John, died when I was a small child, so I only knew him through accounts from my mother. I don't know what became of that tobacco box; I wish I had it as a memento. But I do have his well-worn genuine leather coin purse as an heirloom. Mother spoke of him often and, thus, I felt as though I knew him well.

He began life in his new country as a farm laborer. Later he became a farmer, a landowner, and finally, a businessman as owner and operator of a livery stable, a relatively lucrative enterprise in that era. As a one-time mail carrier he delivered the mail to rural patrons by sleigh and buggy. My mother told me that he was active in politics and held various public offices, serving as deputy sheriff and later sheriff of McPherson County for two terms.

Though stern, he exercised compassion when circumstances permitted it in a rugged era when violence was common. On occasion Sheriff Stock would put a prisoner on his honor and allow him to spend the night as a "guest" in his home. In one case, a man who had been sentenced to serve time in the penitentiary in Sioux Falls, South Dakota, spent more than a week in the Stock home while he awaited orders. This caused his family a certain amount of unease. Stories such as these made him seem to me a fascinating character. I wish he had lived longer so I could have known him.

John Stock
(Photo courtesy of Joan Froh)

I later learned of many other of Grandfather Stock's activities. They included service on the district board of education, deputy county assessor, city alderman, and a director on boards of both a local bank and an investment company. In addition, he served as secretary of the NW German Farmers Mutual Insurance Company for sixteen years until his retirement. This company, with headquarters in Eureka, still exists today. To be successful in all these endeavors, this man who spoke only German when he arrived in 1889 had to teach himself to speak, read, and write in English. Yes indeed, I think he was a fascinating man and I do wish I could have spent time with him.

Although he had many fine qualities, my grandfather was known to have a rather stubborn streak at times. One instance of this was his strong opposition to build a new, larger Lutheran church in Eureka in the 1920s. The congregation had grown and people felt they needed more space. When they approved the construction, he led a contingent of like-minded persons to form their own church, using a visiting pastor. To the day he died he never attended the new church and is buried in the city cemetery. John had not been settled in Eureka very long when he met my grandmother, Margaretha Becker. They were married on December 29, 1890. At age nineteen she had emigrated from Kassel, South Russia, with her family and arrived in New York aboard the SS Eider on May 10, 1889, less than three weeks after her future husband. Ten children were born to them – seven boys and three girls. Three of the boys died in infancy and one from diphtheria at age eight. My grandfather died at age seventy-three on May 30, 1936, at his home in Eureka.

My mother, Bertha, was born April 3, 1908, in Eureka, the youngest of the Stock children. Raised in the typically strict environment of the German families of that day, she was taught to be well-behaved, reserved, and to respect her elders. Children were always to "mind" and "to be seen and not heard." Mother used to tell me how her much older brothers would tease her mercilessly and at times nearly terrorize her about the "bogey man" and other mythical characters. She would run to her room and cringe under the bed covers in fear. In this environment she became a shy and nervous child, very much attached to her mother whom she would often seek out for comfort.

When Bertha was in her mid-teens her father required her to leave school as she was expected to help at home. The family took in boarders and rented out now-vacant rooms. This was devastating to her because she loved school and was an excellent student. Shortly before her nineteenth birthday she married my father, Walter Froh, of Eureka. He had been trained as a printer by his father, Otto H. Froh, who published the local paper.

In 1936 we moved to Ashley, North Dakota, where my father became editor and manager of the *Ashley Tribune*. Within a year my mother began to assist at the newspaper. The local physician had suggested that working at the paper could provide her with more intellectual stimulation. And so my mother became a businesswoman in an era when few women worked outside the home. Her salary was three dollars per week; the live-in "hired girl" who tended to things at home, was paid four dollars per week!

Mother had always disliked her name. Since she had no middle name to use as a fallback, she chose to be called "Bert." She soon became an integral part of the newspaper business—gathering local news, proofreading, editing copy. She even learned to operate the large printing press. To do this, she had to stand on an elevated platform and perfectly time feeding the sheets of newsprint into the huge rotating cylinder. Always precise and good at numbers, Bert became the *Tribune* bookkeeper and financial manager. For a short time in the early 1960s she wrote a popular column titled "Just Chatting." Much of her material was based on reminiscences of growing up in Eureka. She included accounts of German Russian traditions, customs, stories, and anecdotes, plus descriptions of their ethnic foods. I've included two segments of her columns that are particularly relevant even in our present day.

"Remember in the olden days when $10.00 worth of groceries would fill a pantry to bursting? Today, $10.00 worth of groceries won't even burst a shopping bag." If the dates and numbers were changed to 2013, we could say things haven't changed all that much, have they?

Here are a few words from another column that are especially relevant to our present concerns: *"I wonder how many of our younger generation, those of German parentage, know the history of their ancestors?"*

She continues with a somewhat lengthy history explaining where in Germany they came from, why they went to Russia, and what brought them to America. There are several columns with discussions on German food. One fascinating column goes to great length on the art of making strudels, and another about *"fauled Kaese,"* evidently a very smelly, but tasty cheese food. I truly cherish copies of my mother's columns in my possession.

Bertha Stock Froh at work.

(Photo courtesy of Joan Froh)

Thursday night was "press night" at the paper. During summer vacations and holidays, I would sometimes join the staff when they were "putting the paper to bed," as the expression went. What I most enjoyed is when around eleven p.m. we would all go to the local café for a lunch break. When I got sleepy I would nestle down under an old blanket on a cot, and sleep while they finished, usually about eight a.m., and go home. When I was in high school I sometimes wrote articles about school news for the paper. Life was interesting for me growing up in a newspaper environment.

My mother became an excellent writer even though she never had the opportunity to extend her formal education, nor was schooled in journalism. She was bright, articulate, and well-read. Inquisitive and with a sensitive nature, she always took great interest in people. She particularly enjoyed speaking in German with the elderly citizens of the area and sharing stories of their common heritage. Through all of these outlets, my mother gradually became quite outgoing and a good conversationalist. She grew and stretched as a person despite her very strict German Russian upbringing. Bertha Froh passed away at age seventy-six on July 30, 1984. She is buried in the Lutheran cemetery in Ashley, North Dakota.

Both my grandfather, Johann Stock, and his daughter Bertha, my mother, overcame difficult circumstances early in life on the way to becoming successful, productive members of their respective communities. It is with a good deal of pride that I have recorded these memories of their stories.

Nickel Candy Bar

Bernelda Kallenberger Becker

When I was about twelve, we lived in Eureka, South Dakota. I'd been a "farm kid" before. Now my life had changed. I felt I had moved up in the world. My friend Alice and I spent the days entertaining ourselves wandering the streets of our little town. Sometimes we even had a nickel to spend. This meant I wasn't completely dependent on sneaking brown sugar from the pantry when the craving for something sweet could not be overcome, or sneaking into my parents' bedroom to search in the little cedar chest on the dresser for the big, black licorice stick in an orange box that Daddy kept there. I think they used it for medicinal purposes. I'd nibble off a bite. It was not sweet, but you compromise when you are desperate. I also searched my father's linty suit pockets for loose SenSen. He used it as a breath freshener. It tasted sort of like licorice, too.

When I did have a nickel in the early 40s, I could go to the candy counter in the Eureka Bazaar and purchase a small bag of loose candy for that same nickel. There, at the counter, I faced the agony of decision. Maybe a Bit O'Honey bar? It was wrapped in such a way as to be in several pieces and I would be able to carry it home and make it last. I loved "Whiz, the best nickel candy bar there is," a sort of caramel base, with marshmallow, and peanuts all covered over with chocolate. Alas, it was one of those that never made it home.

Maybe a package of gum? There were five sticks of gum in the package. I recall such flavors as Spearmint, Beech Nut, and Juicy Fruit, but my favorite was Black Jack—it had a licorice taste. You could chew on one stick for a whole day, even though the flavor didn't last that long. Maybe I'd buy a box of Cracker Jack. The prizes back then were of higher quality than they are now.

Sometimes I bought hard candy, like root beer barrels. When all you have is five cents, and what you buy must last a week, the choice has to be something that delivers. Candy bars tasted wonderful for the short time they lasted, but I never made it home with one. However if I chose hard candy, I could make it last almost a week. In root beer barrels the flavor was all through the candy. They were big, too. I could suck on one for an hour or so, put it in a safe place for a while, and return for some more good flavor more than once. If I didn't finish it that day, when I came across it a day or a week later, it was just as good as the day I started it. My first and probably only venture into a life of crime came as the result of lusting after a Hershey bar in the Eureka Bazaar. (Yes, they've been around that long!) One day, Alice and I had spent several minutes gazing hungrily at the bars behind the glass candy case. We had no money. The clerk was busy elsewhere and paid us no attention. I can't remember how it came about that we were able to reach the bars, but we each grabbed one and ran. Mine dropped as, heart thumping, I made a mad dash through the door, and I did not have the nerve to go back for it. My life of crime ended then and there.

Hershey bars are still around, and yes, every now and then I yield to temptation. No, I don't grab one and run, but on impulse I drop it into my cart. The very reason the store displays them there is to tempt me, and it still works!

Saving the Day

Penny Eberhart

In the German Russian tradition, there were individuals (men and women) trained in the German faith-healing tradition known as *Brauche*, who had the ability to heal the sick. These healers, who inherited their power and secret remedies from their mothers, were very important persons in German Russian communities, especially before there were many medical doctors available. However in later years, people would still come to see a *Braucher* when medical expertise did not provide help for their ailments. Such was the case for us.

About 1971, my husband, Emil, and I lived in Colome, South Dakota, with our two children. While we were there, our three-year-old daughter, Cathy, developed ringworm the size of a dinner plate on her chest. None of the medications which were prescribed got rid of the ringworm.

That fall we went up to my hometown, Ashley, North Dakota, where my parents, Reinhold and Loretta (Sackmann) Kramer, still lived. When they became aware of the situation, they suggested we go to the local *Brauchere*, Mrs. Eva Iszler, to see if she could help. I don't recall exactly what happened, but I do remember she went into a back room where she did her preparations, and when she returned, she gave us a salve which got rid of the ringworm in a few days.

In 1972 we moved to Arlington, South Dakota, where our daughter Cathy, now five, began to attend kindergarten. Shortly after our third child was born, I noticed that Cathy was scratching her head, but this didn't seem too unusual. However, when she continually rubbed her eyes, I thought it was time to take her to the local doctor. He examined her and without saying a word, he took down a medical book from his shelf, turned to a page and showed me a picture of a louse (he couldn't even say the word). Our daughter had lice not only in her hair, but also in her eye lashes!

116

In those days, the school system did not provide information about this common affliction among children, so I felt awful – like a horrible mother and housekeeper. Our doctor then prescribed some medication. Since I was at home with a small baby and two other children, the druggist offered to deliver the medication to our home. When he arrived, he would not come into our home – he held out his hand a distance from the door and gave me the package.

Now, I really felt bad – like we had leprosy! We began to use the medication to not only wash her hair, but the hair of everyone in the family. But there was one problem – the medication could not be safely used near her eyes.

This happened in mid-December of that year. So when we went to my parents' home for Christmas, they again suggested we go to see Mrs. Iszler. As at our previous visit, I don't remember the details, except when she returned from the back room, she gave us a powder which was safe to use not only in the hair but also on the eye lashes. Before Cathy returned to school after New Year's, the lice were gone.

In the early homestead years, the *Brauchere* were sometimes criticized by the local clergy who accused them of practicing witchcraft. We did not have those suspicions, for we knew that these women were people of deep faith and trust in God. Each of their German verses usually ended with the words *Gott der Vater, Gott der Sohn, Gott der Heilige Geist* (God the Father, God the Son, God the Holy Ghost). Mrs. Iszler has since died, but we are so grateful for her and for how God worked through her to provide healing for our daughter when the medical doctors could not.

[The *Brauche* tradition used a combination of healing potions and religious incantations. It was taught as an oral tradition to a selected individual by a current practicing *Braucher*. During the period of emigration to the U.S. it was commonly passed from mother to daughter. Ed.]

Salomea Job Dockter, *Brauche* and midwife, circa 1920s.
(Photo courtesy of Carol Just)

CHAPTER SIX

Full Circle

Children scrubbing cucumbers at annual family "Pickling Day"
at the Just Farm, rural Berlin, North Dakota, 2012.
(Photo courtesy of Katharina Schirg)

Growing up German from Russia

Nancy Gertner

I was in my forties before I realized that my immigrant great-grandparents Gärtner had renounced their allegiance to Czar Alexander II of Russia to become naturalized American citizens. It took an invitation to the Gertner family reunion from my cousin Willis near the end of the twentieth century to open my eyes to that fact. How could I not have known where my ancestors came from? Their origins were recorded in the Cottonwood County Centennial history book in every library in the county.

My grandfather Herman Gertner was born in 1882, sixteen years after his parents, Elisabeth Hochbaum and Wilhelm Friedrich Gärtner, arrived in New York, just a week before Independence Day in 1876. My grandfather died ten years before I was born, so I never sat on his knee to hear stories of the olden days. Fortunately, my cousin Lyle Gertner was willing to share stories from his grandfather with me at the Gertner family reunions. Lyle's grandfather was born in the old country, and named Wilhelm Friedrich Gärtner like his father, but he became known as Fred W. Gertner. He was the only child born in the old country that would achieve adulthood. His baby sister, Elisabeth, died on the voyage to America and was buried at sea, two days east of Nova Scotia. The ship's manifest said she was a month old as of the sailing, and also stated that Fred W. was ten months. But Fred turned two shortly after their arrival, so that "error" in under reporting his age was apparently common since children under age two were given free passage. Perhaps that was because the mortality was so high for infants in close quarters on the long journey across the ocean.

My cousin Lyle shared stories of the brutal early winters on the Minnesota prairie. My great-grandfather Fred Gertner Sr. would trek cross-country with a sled from Rosehill Township in Cottonwood County to Heron Lake in Jackson County for supplies, about fifteen miles. He did this on foot, as he apparently found it preferable to taking the horses. The prized horses were taken inside the family home during the worst blizzards, as my great-grandfather knew he could not afford to lose his beasts of burden that pulled the farm implements. The cows were left outside to defend themselves against the elements.

Great-grandmother Elisabeth had more children, giving birth to thirteen babies. She was forty-seven when her last child was born, and she died a month after his birth, leaving Ernest to be adopted by her brother, and growing up a Hochbaum. Ernest was only a decade older than my father, Leo, but Ernest moved to California in the middle of the twentieth century, and I don't believe I ever met him. I began researching my family history after the death of my father, so searched for ancestors in records. The older cousins can be very helpful when one only is the oldest generation in their family.

The Gärtner homestead was adjacent to the Rosehill Emmanuel Lutheran Church, and this must have been convenient for Great-grandmother Elisabeth, as Sunday church may have provided her only weekly contact with other women during the long cold winters. Moving from the old country, where families lived in villages with other women nearby likely caused culture shock, as the Homestead Act required people to live on their farms, so the law mandated this major lifestyle change. This undoubtedly put the church and school at the center of community and social life for isolated families living on the open prairie. Unfortunately, I was unable to obtain the homestead application when I visited the National Archives several years ago, because I later learned the name was spelled Gardner on it, and could not find the claim number without using that surname spelling.

Great-grandmother Elisabeth's parents, Katharina Deutschmann and Peter David Hochbaum, had immigrated a year earlier (1875), so Great-grandmother Elisabeth had Hochbaum family including all her siblings nearby, along with numerous maternal aunts and uncles and cousins of the Deutschmann family. Great-grandfather Gärtner's family stayed in Russia, with the exception of his brother Gottlieb, who immigrated with him and also homesteaded in Rosehill Township, adopting one daughter.

Digging into the family history to learn more about this family that had come from Russia, I found a book in the library of the county seat, Windom. This Cottonwood County history book published in 1916 contained information including the names of the Gärtner siblings. This indicates contact was maintained with the family for a number of years after leaving Russia. However, the communication with family in the old country probably ended by 1918. The Russian Revolution in 1917 and WWI made both Russian and German ethnicities targets of discrimination. Immigration quotas were drastically reduced for people coming from Eastern Europe. Out of fear of deportation and allegiance to their new country, my immigrant ancestors apparently severed contact with family in the homeland.

It would be over ninety years before emails from Russia and Germany enabled me to establish contact with living descendants of my "left behind" Deutschmann and Gärtner family siblings, now living in Germany after a long journey back via Siberia.

My quest to learn more about my immigrant ancestors led me to seek out people that had done genealogy research. I joined the North Star Chapter (of Germans from Russia), and met Arlene Yochem Ulstad at the annual genealogy workshop meeting. Eureka! Arlene had looked at church records and knew where in Russia my Gärtner family had come from! She shared a wealth of information with me. We shared Grams ancestors, and were later able to determine how her female Gärtner ancestor in Russia was related to my male Gärtner ancestor. Meeting with my cousins, Elmer Deutschmann and Barbara Nelson helped further my research. My family's life events were recorded in the church records of Grunau Lutheran Parish in South Russia. Further research revealed they had lived in West Prussia before migrating to the Black Sea area of Russia in the 1820s and 1830s from farms near Tiegenhof south of the Baltic Sea, now part of Poland.

In 2005, I was privileged to visit this area with Mennonite Heritage Tours. My Deutschmann ancestor who emigrated from Prussia to Russia had married a Mennonite Neufeld woman that he apparently met and married around 1820 from the Molotschna Mennonite colony near Wickerau, where they settled. I learned Mennonite heritage on this tour in addition to seeing the area my ancestors had lived in two hundred years ago, and met some interesting Mennonite people, many from Canada. I appreciated that my great-great-great-grandmother Maria Neufeld Deutschmann had likely been a major influence on her children that decided to immigrate to America in the 1870s. Following custom and law, the Deutschmann farm was passed to the youngest son, Diedrich, who stayed in Russia when his elder siblings left for America. Someday I hope to learn more of Diedrich's family from the survivors in Germany. The Mennonite doctrine of non-violence caused aversion to military service, and when the exemption from service in the Russian military was eliminated in the early 1870s, migration of many Mennonites from Russia to several continents resulted. One of the large Mennonite settlements in the United States was in Mountain Lake, Minnesota, in the eastern part of my own county of birth. The people on my Mennonite Heritage tour had surnames familiar to me from my days in Cottonwood County 4-H.

Browsing through the obituaries in the card catalog at the Minnesota History Center in Saint Paul netted a gem of an obituary for my immigrant great-grandfather Gärtner. Called a "financier" in the 1915 newspaper obituary, my immigrant great-grandfather must have been a very tenacious and hard-working pioneer devoted to setting up all his children in business. He retired to a Victorian home in the new village of Westbrook (established in 1900), living out his final years with his second wife, Wilhelmina Schwendig Braun, who was the widowed mother of his son Edward's wife.

Following the traditions of the Germans in Russia, my immigrant ancestors passed the homestead farm to the youngest son for two generations. Because his youngest brother was adopted by his Hochbaum uncle, Grandfather Herman was the *de facto* youngest, and took possession of the homestead. He married my grandmother Sophia Yahnke in 1907, and they raised three sons on this quarter-section (one hundred sixty acres) farm. The eldest son, Carl, went to work with his uncle Rudolph Yahnke to learn the carpentry trade, and also served in the military during WWII. My father's younger brother Vernon was destined to take over the homestead, so my grandparents helped my father, Leo, get set up in farming.

Fortunately my grandparents had only three children to launch in business, and the year after President Franklin Delano Roosevelt had declared "The only thing we have to fear is fear itself," my grandparents took out a mortgage on their homestead in order to buy a quarter-section farm for my father in 1934. They made monthly payments for ten years on this mortgage of eighty-nine hundred dollars, and records indicate my father finally paid off the debt in the 1950s. Their gamble during the Great Depression could have caused the loss of their farm.

Father and his brothers held an annual sausage-making event when I was young, but this was discontinued during my childhood, and my dad began having the meat market at Jeffers make his sausage. He had a fondness for "head cheese" that my mother would make for him, though she seemed to not share his fondness for the delicacy. Those are the only food customs I remember from childhood that I associate with my father's family. I think we derive most of our food ways from our mother's families.

Father grew up speaking German at home and also spoke German in his confirmation class. His mother's Jahnke family was from Posen Province of Prussia, but they also spoke the *Plattdeutsch* dialect of my Gärtner ancestors from the Grunau district of South Russia. Dad and Grandma frequently spoke German over the phone or in person so they could keep from sharing their conversations with the rest of us. Grandmother had attended Normal School at Wilder, Minnesota, and become a schoolteacher like her older sister Mary Yahnke. Grandmother Sophia married at age twenty-five, which was considerably mature for a bride in 1907. Her father, Johann August Jahnke, served in the Prussian Army, which had a literacy rate over ninety percent, and the Jahnke family placed a high value on education. Great-grandfather Jahnke was the enumerator for Rosehill Township in the state census of 1885, and his handwritten census record revealed a familiarity (he listed Elisabeth as Liza) with my grandfather's parents that indicated Herman and Sophia were perhaps destined to marry since age three or earlier. My parents were also perhaps so destined, growing up a mile apart in Rosehill Township and baptized in the same rural Lutheran church. The Depression and WWII were factors that made for a decade-long courtship, and Flossie Mitchell and Leo Gertner were united in marriage in a June wedding ten days after D-Day in 1944.

And the Wine Was Good

Dallas D. Zimmerman

It was in 1973 that I first learned that my Zimmerman ancestors had immigrated to Russia from a town called Gronau in Germany. The information came unexpectedly from my father's cousin Georg Zimmerman, who now resided in West Germany but had lived in Bessarabia until late 1940. It seems that I have always known that my Zimmerman (and maternal Schlecht) grandparents had immigrated to North Dakota from South Russia - Friedenstal, Bessarabia. As a child I heard this discussed by my parents, uncles, and aunts. However, I don't recall any discussion that my grandparents' grandparents immigrated to Russia from Germany. Perhaps as a youngster I wondered why our family spoke the German language but our ancestors were supposed to have come from Russia. I doubt if I ever asked for an explanation.

In fact, I had little or no curiosity about my roots until I was a senior in college. After almost four years of required chemistry and math courses, I decided to take a North Dakota history course as an easy elective. The NDSU history professor, however, expected his students to study and furthermore prepare a term paper on some historical subject. For reasons unknown, I selected "German Russians in McIntosh County" as my topic. Perhaps after being away from McIntosh County and the German Russian community for several years, I sensed that there was something special about these people. My paper was not a masterpiece. It was in the preparation of the paper, however, that a curiosity about my heritage began. I began to wonder why the Zimmermans happened to become Bessarabians and where their home in Germany might have been.

I was elated when, in March 1976, an opportunity arose for a business trip to Europe. I decided to go to Gronau. Through an aunt in North Dakota I obtained the address of Georg Zimmerman's brother Gerhard, who lived north of Stuttgart, Germany. Georg had died in 1975. I sent a letter to Gerhard inquiring whether I could visit him for a weekend and indicated that I'd like to go to Gronau. I didn't exactly know where the town was situated or what remained of it. A careful search of German maps with the aid of a magnifying glass had been fruitless. Gerhard responded quickly welcoming me to come to his home and informing me that he would take me to Gronau.

I arrived in Stuttgart by train late on a Friday evening and spent the night in a hotel across the street from the station. Gerhard and I met at the station at eight the next morning. There was a concern on my part that we might not be able to find each other since we had no idea what the other looked like. This was not a problem, however, because we quickly spotted each other and instantly recognized each other as a Zimmerman.

I spent the Saturday in Asperg at the home of Gerhard and his family. Gerhard, his wife, Ella, and daughter Wilma had lived in Friedenstal until late 1940. Gerhard told me many things about life in Bessarabia and their experiences during the War. He told of his education, being fluent in German, Romanian and Russian, farming in the 1920s and 30s, doing their genealogy in 1940 to establish that they were Germans, and their relocation to German-occupied Poland. He touched on his stay in the German army and his capture by American troops. He told of his wife's and daughter's flight to the Western Zone as the Russian troops advanced, and how he found his family again. We talked late into the night. Although I had read many articles about the life of the Germans in Russia and their plight during World War II, hearing the story from a relative made everything seem more real. The featherbed was soft and warm but sleep did not come easy that night. It had been a day of excitement and the adrenalin was kept flowing as I thought ahead to the next day. On Sunday we would go to Gronau.

We drove to Gronau early in the afternoon. Gronau is a small town with perhaps one thousand inhabitants. It was a sunny spring day. Our first stop was the cemetery. We walked through the grounds where no doubt the bones of three generations of the Zimmerman family were resting. The grave markers have long since disappeared. After a stop at the Rathaus (City Hall), we headed to the place that had been on my mind for a long time, the Zimmerman home. The place from which Georg Simon Zimmerman, wine gardener and farmer, along with his wife and three children in June 1832, left for Russia. They would settle in Lichtental, Bessarabia, for two years and then move to Friedenstal. Fifty-five year later Georg Simon's great-grandson Gottlieb, my grandfather, would leave Friedenstal for America.

The Zimmerman house was hit by a bomb during the latter part of the war and had to be partially rebuilt. We stopped at the house and were invited in by the present owners. After visiting for a while, we headed up the hill to see the old Zimmerman vineyard. We returned to the house to sample the wine. I recall sitting at the table reflecting on what had transpired the past two days and analyzing my feelings. My feelings were not of intense excitement. The adrenalin was not flowing. My feelings instead were like the feelings that one gets after returning home from a long trip.

Almost seven years have passed since my visit to Gronau. I have been to many places and sampled the finest wines of France, Italy, Australia, and the Rhine. However, I have not found a wine more satisfying than that tasted at the Zimmerman home. For on that March day in Gronau the wine was very good.

Previously published in the Minnesota North Star Chapter, Germans from Russia Newsletter, 1982, and in Vol.13, No 2, May 1983 GRHS Heritage Review.

Half and Half

Sharon Chmielarz

I grew up 50% German Russian. I knew there were differences between my dad and mom, the other 50%. Mom grew up in North Dakota learning German, for instance, at school even though her mother, Margareta, emigrated from Germany when she was eighteen. My dad learned English in a country school in North Dakota. His mother emigrated from Odessa when she was three. My dad was pulled from school after the third grade to help Grandpa in the fields because at ten he could read, Grandpa said, and knew enough math to get by. Mom graduated from a normal school.

Mom referred to a car or vacuum cleaner or cat as "it." For Dad it was always "he" or "she." The moon was a "he", too. Although Dad spoke mostly without an accent (I thought) he always pronounced "h" like "etch" and did battles with the dictionary equaling the fervor of Don Quixote tilting at windmills: how was it possible to find a word in the dictionary when none of the English words looked the way they sounded! The book was absolutely useless when it came to words that made my dad's mouth water. Like *stirrum*, *halupsie*, and *plachinda*. Quite a change for the boy who once threw a fit at the table because all they ate was *plachinda*. For me it was potatoes. Mashed, mashed, mashed, boiled, fried, and mashed. I was so sick of eating potatoes I swore I'd never eat one again when I grew up. (Another vow broken.)

But I didn't think I was different. Didn't every kid call her grandparents by their last name? Grandpa Grenz. Grandma Grenz. And shake their hands when they visited? Or get poked in the ribs when playing with cousins who said funny things like, "Gel, Sharon?" and at the table, "*Oboy. Wassermelone.*"

By the time I reached eighth grade I realized my dad was one of the "German Roosians" like the people who lived in Java and Selby, Hosmer and Eureka, whose accents the town kids made fun of. I intuited a class difference that made the German Russians in my town low on the social totem pole. Rationally this made no sense at all. There were plenty of people with a Germans from Russia background who held rather high positions. But who can argue with uncontested logic? I started denying half of my family despite the fact that one of my childhood's fondest memories was of my grandfather and me.

He and Grandma drove down to Mobridge, South Dakota, from the farm at Fredonia, North Dakota, for a rare visit. They were both dressed in their Sunday best, of course, because they were visiting. Grandma, out of her apron and into a longish dark dress and little black hat, and Grandpa in a suit which included a vest. I caught him standing at the front yard gate alone, humming under his breath. I joined him and babbled away beside his shiny dark green 4-door Dodge (late 40s? early 50s?) parked in the street outside our house. The next thing I knew he was digging in his change-purse and fingering out a quarter. For me! A little girl doesn't forget an unexpected moment like that.

It would be the first and last present I'd ever receive from them. (Compare that to today's grandchildren.) When I asked my older sister Marilyn what he gave her, she half-pretended huffiness. "That's more than I ever got." But truly we didn't expect any presents. Certainly not on a birthday, and at Christmas only from Santa/our parents.

From high school on 50% of me disappeared. What stuck, I deliberately ignored. One problem though. Even over the first-class chip on my shoulder, I kept seeing references to Germans from Russia. Annie Proulx, for instance, includes them in her novel *The Accordion*. "And she's not even German Russian," I thought, as if she were infringing on my rights. Maybe I couldn't value it, but other people found the trek the German Russians took to the United States unique as were their communities, with the earliest having an all-Catholic core or Lutheran or Mennonite, etc.

Food didn't lure me back to my German Russian 50%. I could live without my grandmother's meals of sausage, fresh bread, pound cake that weighed at least two pounds (How many eggs did she use anyway?) and canned fruit sauce for dessert. In one of my sister Marilyn's richest memories she's gawking at Grandma Grenz slicing bread–holding the round loaf on her hip and wielding a sharp knife like a surgeon. I could live without *Kuchen* for it held few memories of other kinds of communication between my paternal grandmother and me. I doubt she spoke very much English; maybe none at all. And I didn't speak German. What I remember is her shaking her head over something my dad and Grandpa were talking about and saying, "Ei, yei, YEI, yei, yei, yei, yei, yei, yei." Or, "Donnerwetter noch einmal." THAT was one phrase I loved to repeat in the back seat on the way home after a visit. Donnerwetternocheinmal. Just run all the sounds and words together. Didn't matter what it meant. I sure didn't know. But it was fun. Sing it! Was my grandma swearing? Cool! Donnerwetternocheinmal.

No, food didn't bring me back to 100%. It was appreciation of German Russian history and acceptance of myself and my past. As Popeye says, "I yam what I yam." And by the way, I can now speak German. The wrong kind, but hey! I'm halfway there, too.

Fleischküchle at the Dairy Queen

Cynthia Miller

When I was about four years old, my grandma and I were walking down the street in my prairie hometown of Beulah, North Dakota. One of the old German ladies stopped to greet my grandma and observed me, with my waist-length brown hair and big blue eyes, placidly sucking my thumb.

"Oh, ya, you're sucking your tum?" she asked, with an accent that even being born in America didn't quite erase.

I pulled my thumb out of my mouth with a snap and said clearly, "No! It's called a 'thumb'!" My grandma was horrified at my lack of manners. I'm not sure she would've been comforted in that moment to look into the future and see that I became an English teacher. I teach writing part-time at a business college and sometimes my students want to know how old I am. A lady doesn't reveal her age – except for my grandma, who everyone knows is thirty-nine – so I give my students a math and a history lesson. I tell them I was born sometime between Kennedy's assassination and the moon landing. That means I grew up in the 70s and 80s, at the top of the Sauerkraut Triangle. I'm 100% German from Russia on both sides, and I've been coming to terms with that since the day I was born.

As often happens, I've learned a lot more about who I am and where I'm from since I grew up and moved away. I know that my ancestors – unlike some immigrant groups – were very successful in their homeland, and left partly because of their persecution for that success. I know they recreated their lives in Russia here in the upper Midwest by settling in strong communities, based in faith and family, and by working hard to achieve the same success, often within a generation.

When I was researching my master's thesis on the German Russian newspapers in the Midwest, I looked at the names of some of the people who lived in the same villages in Russia that my great-grandparents had lived in. There were Unruhs and Boeckels and Weigums, and I thought that was sort of neat, because those were the names of people I knew in Beulah. Then I looked further back at Württemburg, where my ancestors had lived in Germany, and again, there were those same names. I thought, my goodness, I've been living next door to these people for over two hundred years.

That was the way it was when I grew up, even as second- and third-generation Americans. In Beulah, you heard German spoken in the streets. My third grade teacher, an Irish Catholic, would end whatever instruction she was giving by saying, "*Verstehe*? (Understand)" I learned to sing "*Du, du, liegst mir im Herzen*" and "*O Tannenbaum*" before I knew what they meant. We could go to the Dairy Queen and order *Fleischküchle*. I thought everyone in America ate it.

I heard a lot of German spoken in my family. My parents understood it pretty well, but for us kids, we mainly heard German when something was being said that they didn't want us to understand. My grandparents had the curious habit of yelling at us in German if we did something wrong. We knew we were in trouble but we didn't know why. The aunts and uncles used the language to their own advantage, telling us kids to say something naughty in German to shock someone, which we would willingly and innocently do, so they could have a hearty laugh. My grandma once lamented that I didn't know German.

"Why didn't you teach it to Dad then, or me?" I asked, exasperated.

"I don't know," she mused. "I suppose it was America so we wanted to use English."

I was fortunate to have great-grandparents still alive until I was a teenager. We visited them frequently since they all lived in the same county. I didn't enjoy it much as a child because everyone sat around speaking German, they wouldn't let us turn on the TV, and the only candy Grossmama had was sticky orange foam peanuts. My parents had over 50 first cousins between them so it's not surprising that even in my relatively small high school class of 50 students, I had two classmates who were my second cousins. I couldn't have been more surrounded by German Russian culture unless I transported myself back to the Black Sea.

But there were many times when I didn't want to be German. It seemed so boring and ordinary. Everywhere I looked there were Germans, except for the few Norwegians who were let in to town. The biggest event of the year was Wiener and Sauerkraut Day in October, and I didn't like wieners or sauerkraut. Actually, I don't like much traditional German Russian food, except for *halvah* (a Turkish treat that found its way to the Russian Steppes and then halfway across the world to the American Midwest). I was not spoiled though; when we went to Sunday dinner at Grandma's and German food was on the table, I got shown the bread and butter. It was only as an adult that I learned to enjoy *Kuchen* because I found out it could be made with something other than rhubarb and sour cream.

By the time I got to high school, I decided I wanted to study German because I wanted to finally know what my grandparents were saying. My high school was small, and every year I would sign up for German, and every year there wasn't enough interest to hold a class. The only foreign language that my school offered was French. That might seem puzzling, but by the 1980s, Beulah was changing. The town of three thousand mostly Germans from Russia descendants almost doubled in size within ten years because of the construction of a synthetic fuels plant. People moved in from all over the country and the world. I remember a girl from South Africa sitting behind me in class, passing me an English-Afrikaans dictionary so I could help her speak with our teacher. These outsiders may have enjoyed our quaint food but they didn't care much about who we were and where we'd come from. Many were only there a few months, a tiny jump stop on their families' journeys. They didn't know we'd made big journeys as well, coming halfway around the world, resettling twice on two different continents.

When I got to college, I was finally able to sign up for German. It was the first college class I ever attended. We were a bunch of freshmen, away from home for the first time, and our professor took pity on us that day. The first word we learned was *Heimweh*, which she translated as "home hurt." Frau Zerr-Peltner was from Linton, North Dakota, and she knew that many of us would better understand a *Schwäbisch* dialect. But she said she couldn't teach us that because it wasn't proper German. I took one course every term – even visited Germany for the first time during my junior year – and earned a minor in German. But this didn't help when, shortly before I graduated, I was in a store and a little girl held up a fruit-shaped soap and asked, "*Ist das zu essen?*" I hurriedly said, "*Nein, nicht zu essen.*" She started rattling off German so fast that I couldn't understand another word. Her grandmother joined us and explained that she was from Germany, this was her first visit to America, and she didn't understand that no one spoke German. I was depressed because I realized after five years of study, I didn't have the language ability to match a four-year-old child.

I've never quite gotten over feeling inadequate as a German from Russia because of my lack of language ability. It's part of the reason why I send my half-German children to German immersion schools. Perhaps that's why I've tried so hard to discover and understand as much of my culture as I could without major use of the language. For many years, I was one of the few people at the national Germans from Russia conventions who still had her natural hair color (I don't anymore). Understanding my culture, coming to terms with what is familiar and what is almost unimaginable, has become a life's mission for me. People who study immigration patterns tell us it's natural and good for people to become absorbed in their new culture and lose their old ties. I don't believe it for a minute. You can still get *Fleischküchle* at my hometown Dairy Queen, and even that once-detested childhood food is now a treat that takes me back to my grandma's kitchen, and gives me some sense of who I am in this world.

Rodeo Days parade down Main Street, Beulah, North Dakota, 1948.
(Photo courtesy of Edith Christman)

Author Bios

Bernelda Kallenberger Becker was born in Eureka, South Dakota. Interest in her heritage began with an article in the *Minneapolis StarTribune* about the 1996 AHSGR Convention in Bloomington, Minnesota. Attending it launched Bernie into unearthing her rich and interesting heritage. She joined the North Star Chapter of Minnesota (Germans from Russia) and discovered their library, the AHSGR and GRHS archives, and new friends. Retired, Bernie writes for Christian publications and secular magazines. Her ancestral villages in Russia are Neuberg, Kassel, and Guildendorf.

Sharon Grenz Chmielarz has had eight books of poetry published. Her work has been a finalist in the National Poetry Series and also nominated often for a Pushcart Prize. Her father was a Grenz from the Fredonia, North Dakota, area. You can hear her read poems at www.sharonchmielarz.com.

Penelope (Penny) Kramer Eberhart grew up in Lehr and Ashley, North Dakota. She was a home economics teacher and later became an ordained United Methodist pastor serving churches in South Dakota. Penny and her husband, Emil, live in Oak Park Heights, Minnesota. Penny's emigrant ancestors emigrated from the Wittenberg and Bergdorf areas of South Russia, coming to the United States in 1892 and 1903.

Joan Froh was born in Eureka, South Dakota, but grew up just across the border in Ashley, North Dakota. She received BS and MS degrees in education and taught science, health, and physical education in Minnesota public schools, largely in suburbs of Minneapolis. Now retired, she lives in Richfield, Minnesota. It was through her mother, Bertha Froh, that Joan developed an interest in researching her German from Russia heritage.

Born in Cottonwood County in southwestern Minnesota, **Nancy Gertner** attended Shady Nook School, a one-room country school adjacent to the family farm in Rosehill Township in the 1960s. After completing her public education, she served in the United States Navy. Now retired, Nancy owns and is restoring Shady Nook School. Nancy's immigrant Lutheran Gärtner ancestors lived in the Grunau District of the Black Sea area of Russia and came to Minnesota in 1875 and 1876.

James Gessele is a native North Dakotan of German Russian descent. He received his BA from Concordia College, Moorhead, Minnesota, and MAT in German from Stanford University. After a career in teaching, including a four-year stint teaching English in a German grammar school, he entered civil engineering and retired in 2001 when he took up translating as a hobby. Two of his works have been published; several more are in development. He has served as editor of the GRHS quarterly, *Heritage Review.*

John Hafner lives in the Twin Cities. Following service in the United States Navy as a radar electronics technician, John worked as a factory service representative. Now retired, John works part-time as a shuttle driver for a car rental agency. As pastoral assistant and tenor in the Berea Lutheran church choir, John continues to serve in the church his parents pastored from its beginning. He loves fishing and traveling with his wife. John and his cousins plan to travel to Sarata, Ukraine, in the fall of 2014.

Shirley Keller Halvorsen grew up in a German Russian community in western Nebraska. Her parents' families emigrated from Frank, Russia, in the early 1900s. They settled in the Scottsbluff, Nebraska, area to farm, mainly sugar beets. It was an experience of a lifetime for Shirley to travel to Russia in 1985 to visit relatives and gain an insight into her ancestry and heritage. Shirley lives in Houston, Texas, with her husband, Marc.

Elvera Hepner Hofmann grew up on a dairy farm in McLeod County, Minnesota. She helped with chores, animals, flowers, and gardening. All of Elvera's Germans from Russia relatives were loyal and committed to one another. After a career as a lab technician, Elvera married and raised three daughters who now live in Texas, California, and Minnesota. "My trip to Russia in 1995 will always be with me – heart and soul," Elvera says.

Dr. Chris L Huber was born in Eureka, South Dakota, and was baptized at St. John's Lutheran Church, rural McPherson County. He attended Wartburg College in Waverly, Iowa, where he earned his BA degree and met his wife, Marlene Deutschmann. He subsequently earned a MA and PhD. and served most of his professional career in Minnesota. His maternal and paternal parentage originated in the village of Glückstal, South Russia.

Born and raised in Berlin, LaMoure County, North Dakota, **Carol Just** has been researching her family history since she was a teenager. She is an oral historian with a degree in history. All of her great-grandparents emigrated from the Glückstal Colonies and Bessarabia in South Russia in the 1880s. Carol has traveled to her ancestral villages in Ukraine, Bessarabia, Germany, Alsace, and Poland. She is a founding member of the North Star Chapter of Minnesota (Germans from Russia).

Jake Klotzbeacher (1912 – 2003) was a founding member of the North Star Chapter of Minnesota (Germans from Russia). He served as the first chapter librarian, delivering the boxes of books to every meeting in the back of his shiny Ford Thunderbird. Jake and his wife, Ethel, hosted board and committee meetings, organized events, and were tireless supporters of Germans from Russia research. With his trademark handlebar mustache and clever wit, Jake may be gone, but will not be forgotten.

Andy Kroneberger was born at Remsen, Iowa, in 1928. His family moved to a farm near Brewster, Minnesota, in 1936. He attended St John's University, served in the United States Army from 1951 to 1953, and is a retired NY Life Insurance agent and underwriter. Married to Joyce since 1951, they raised five children. In 2010, Andy published the story of his father's 1912 emigration from Deller (Beresowska), Russia, near the Volga River: *A Man Called Andreas.*

Rosemary Wiesner Larson grew up on a farm in Ellis County, Kansas. After attending schools in the area, she worked as a receptionist. She married her husband, Ken, in 1953, and they have five children. They owned their own business as importers and distributers of Swiss sewing machines. Rosemary is a charter member of the North Star Chapter and served for many years as chapter treasurer, AHSGR Board and Foundation member, and Volga Colonies Village Coordinator.

Born in 1929, **Hertha Bieber Lutz** spent her first eighteen years on a farm just east of Hosmer, South Dakota. Her ancestors emigrated from the Black Sea colonies in 1890 and 1907. Hertha left Hosmer in 1947, spent one year at Wartburg College in Iowa, then worked with a Lutheran national office in Columbus, Ohio. Her entire work life was given to non-profit agencies. She and her husband, Charles Lutz, married fifty-eight years, have three children, six grandchildren, and one great-grandchild.

Cynthia Miller grew up in Beulah, North Dakota, surrounded by her Germans from Russia heritage. She holds bachelor's degrees in mass communications and political science from Minnesota State University Moorhead and a master's degree in journalism from Iowa State University. Her thesis was a study of German-language newspapers in the Midwest published for Germans from Russia immigrants. She is a writer, speaker, and college instructor, and lives in the Twin Cities with her husband, son, Gus, and daughter, Susanna.

Patsy Ramberg's German Russian families are the Graf/Bucks from Streeter, North Dakota, and the Baiers from Harvey, North Dakota. Patsy is a retired teacher who now writes and knits. Her most recent book is *The Farm at Pony Gulch* which tells of the Baier homestead near Harvey, published in 2012 by the Germans from Russia Heritage Center (GRHC) at North Dakota State University (NDSU), Fargo, North Dakota.

Merv Rennich grew up in McClusky, North Dakota. He attended the University of North Dakota at Grand Forks then worked for Caterpillar Tractor Company with various overseas assignments. Merv's father was born in Waterloo, Cherson District, South Russia, and came to the United States in 1909. Merv's mother's family came from Hoffnungstal, Bessarabia, in 1903, all settling in Mercer, North Dakota. Retired, Merv enjoys playing in a German polka band, doing genealogy research, writing, traveling, and visiting grandchildren.

Dallas Zimmerman (1937-2013) was born on a farm south of Lehr, McIntosh County, North Dakota. Both paternal Zimmerman and maternal Schlecht ancestors came to Dakota Territory from Friedenstal, Bessarabia. Zimmerman was a founding member of the North Star Chapter of Minnesota (Germans from Russia).

CPSIA information can be obtained at www.ICGtesting.com
Printed in the USA
LVOW11s0549270614

391882LV00001B/1/P